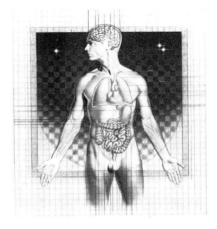

Diagnosis and Treatment
of Anxiety Disorders:

A Physician's Handbook

Thomas J. McGlynn, MD
Harry L. Metcalf, MD

Editors

Art Director:
Fredi White

Associate Art Director:
Ann-Marie Fagnoni

Cover Illustration:
Steve Heimann

Contents

The manifestations of anxiety have long been a familiar part of every primary care practice. All too often, they have also been a source of frustration to the practitioner. Anxiety symptoms can be chronic and disabling. They can complicate other illnesses, often decreasing patient cooperation with treatment regimens and worsening outcome. Moreover, in the absence of clear guidelines, the symptoms of anxiety can appear vague, diffuse, and undefined.

Fortunately, the prevailing picture of anxiety disorders is coming into clearer focus today, facilitating the development of a new approach to anxious patients—one that can transform the frustrations of the past into opportunities. This new approach is based on the following developments and perspectives:

- Precise diagnostic criteria can facilitate the differentiation of specific anxiety disorders from other disorders or the stress and strain of everyday life.
- Significant advances have improved our understanding of the biological correlates of anxiety disorders.
- An increasing variety of effective treatment strategies—both pharmacologic and nonpharmacologic—are now available for each anxiety disorder.
- Primary care physicians usually have first—and sometimes the only—access to anxious patients and are, in most cases, the most appropriate providers of treatment.
- With appropriate treatment, most patients get better.

The new approach to anxious patients is presented in this Handbook in a practical, easily accessible format. Part One discusses general principles of diagnosis and treatment of anxiety disorders from the primary care physician's perspective. Part Two provides a detailed description of diagnostic criteria and management strategies for each anxiety disorder. The Appendices include examples of assessment tools as well as reproducible patient information aids.

This Handbook was prepared by a panel of primary care physicians and psychiatrists selected because of their knowledge, interest, and clinical experience with anxiety disorders. It has one purpose: to present the new approach to anxious patients so that more people can be helped.

Part One: New Approach to Anxious Patients

A WORD ON INTERVIEWING

When it comes to interviewing patients with anxiety disorders, physicians express a variety of concerns:

- "It takes too much time."

- "I don't want to open Pandora's box."

- "I won't know what to do once I've identified the problem."

- "I'm not comfortable working with patients who have psychogenic symptoms; that's the job of a psychiatrist."

Patients have a different set of concerns:

- "I hope the doctor will take the time to listen to me and not rush me out of the office."

- "I hope the doctor will take my symptoms seriously."

- "I hope the doctor won't say my symptoms are all in my head."

- "I hope the doctor doesn't find anything seriously wrong with me."

Physicians are as concerned with meeting time constraints as patients are with being allowed enough time to be heard. If the interview is focused and structured, the demands of both can be met. A key factor in time management is deciding early on what must be known today and what can wait until the next visit or the one after that. The physician and the patient should negotiate a realistic agenda early in the interview. Concerns of both that fall outside the scope of the proposed agenda can be addressed at subsequent visits.

The typical primary care physician sees at least one patient every day with an anxiety disorder. In fact, anxiety disorders are more common than diabetes mellitus in the primary care office. Primary care physicians need to know how to recognize, treat, or refer patients with anxiety disorders, because such patients are far more likely to see a primary care physician than they are a psychiatrist. This section reviews an approach to diagnosing patients with anxiety-based symptoms.

PATIENT PRESENTATION

Some patients with anxiety disorders present their symptoms in psychological terms ("I can't cope," "I can't do my job," "I feel nervous," etc.). Many attribute their symptoms to physical causes and often focus their complaints on one body system. Even patients who suspect an emotional cause may be reluctant to say so. They may believe that physicians are interested only in body system disorders and may feel that emotional problems are a sign of weakness.

Many anxious patients do not meet strict criteria for an anxiety disorder diagnosis when they first present. They are often seen at early stages in the illness and will not have experienced or may ignore some of the characteristic symptoms. Nevertheless, primary care physicians are in an excellent position to provide therapeutic intervention early on, before the symptoms become truly disabling.

Because anxiety disorders generate multisystem symptoms, diagnosing an anxiety disorder requires the same general approach that is used in diagnosing any other illness. However, acquiring the specific skills necessary to recognize and effectively treat anxious patients involves updating the way physicians think about anxiety disorders.

Knowledge of the constellations of symptoms that comprise the anxiety disorders provides the essential background. The medical interview is the means by which that knowledge is put into action and the forum in which the physician-patient relationship begins.

THE IMPORTANCE OF THE INTERVIEW

The medical interview is the physician's major means of establishing a therapeutic relationship with the patient.[1-3] Most patient contact occurs during the inter-

Table 1
Symptoms of Anxiety

Symptoms associated with panic disorder:*

- Choking sensation or "lump in the throat"
- Skipping, racing, or pounding of the heart
- Excessive sweating
- Rubbery or "jelly" legs
- Nausea or abdominal distress
- Trembling or shaking
- Difficulty in getting one's breath, smothering sensations, overbreathing
- Chest pain, pressure, or discomfort
- Faintness, light-headedness, or dizziness
- Feeling off balance or unsteady
- Tingling or numbness in parts of the body
- Hot flashes or chills
- Preoccupation with health concerns
- Feeling that things in the environment are strange, unreal, foggy, or detached
- Feeling outside or detached from all or part of the body, having a floating feeling
- Fear of dying or that something terrible is about to happen
- Feeling of losing control or going insane
- Agoraphobic avoidance behavior
- Feeling frightened suddenly and unexpectedly for no immediately apparent reason

Symptoms associated with other anxiety disorders:†

- Trouble swallowing or "lump in throat"
- Increased heart rate
- Sweaty palms
- Weakness in the knees
- Fluttery stomach, nausea, diarrhea
- Trembling, twitching, feeling shaky
- Shortness of breath
- Tense, uptight feeling
- Inability to relax
- Muscle tension, aches, soreness
- Dry mouth
- Frequent urination
- Exaggerated startle response
- Difficulty concentrating or "mind going blank"
- Trouble falling or staying asleep
- Irritability or impatience

*Symptoms occur in discrete episodes and may eventually lead to avoidance behavior.

†Symptoms tend to be continuous rather than episodic.

view. The outcome of the interview often determines such vital issues as patient cooperation, trust, comprehension, and satisfaction on the part of both the physician and the patient. The interview serves several functions simultaneously:

- It defines the problem(s).

- It determines the accuracy and completeness of historical data.

- It creates expectations for both the physician and the patient concerning the illness and the chief complaint(s).

- It allows for the joint creation of an agenda for the intervention and care to follow.

In short, the medical interview is the foundation for putting the new approach to anxious patients into practice.

SIX STEPS TO DIAGNOSING AN ANXIETY DISORDER

Diagnosing an anxiety disorder consists essentially of the following six steps:

Step 1: Listen. The first and most important step in diagnosis is to listen to the patient—not just to the words, but to what those words mean to the patient. Give patients adequate time to describe their symptoms, the circumstances under which they occur, any aggravating factors, the evolution of associated symptoms, and other important characteristics. Avoid prematurely shaping the patient's story into a familiar medical diagnosis.

The average primary care physician allows a patient an average of only 18 seconds before interrupting during the interview.[4] An effective technique is to give the patient enough time to complete an opening statement. The chief (or first-mentioned) complaint, however, may not always be the most important. Patients often reserve discussing sensitive subjects until they feel more at ease.

As the patient talks, listen for patterns—of symptoms, behavior, and emotional intonation. Keep in mind that anxiety may account for symptoms in the cardiac, pulmonary, gastrointestinal, or central or peripheral nervous system. Consider the most likely diagnoses first. An uncommon presentation of a common disorder (such as an anxiety disorder) is more likely to explain the patient's symptoms than is a common presentation of an uncommon disorder (such as pheochro-

mocytoma). Unless features of the patient's presentation suggest a physical disorder, don't postpone consideration of a likely and treatable anxiety disorder in order to rule out unlikely disorders with time-consuming, unnecessary, and costly laboratory studies. However, even if an underlying physical disorder is unlikely to be the explanation for the symptoms, the physician must keep an open mind to other less common disorders that can mimic an anxiety disorder.

Let the patient tell the story of the illness while you receive, store, and ponder the information being provided. Guide the course of the narrative without interfering with the patient's story. This is the time to use open-ended questions, such as "What happened then?" or "Tell me more about that," leaving the patient free to talk without bias or limits. Suggest that the patient go back to the beginning of the illness or episode, by inquiring "When did you last feel completely well?" or "When did you first notice these symptoms?" Patients with anxiety disorders often can remember the circumstances of their first episode quite clearly.

Step 2: Inquire. Once you have heard the patient's story and generated hypotheses, gather additional specific information. This is the time to use focused questions. "Tell me more about the chest pain." "What made it better?" "Worse?" Questions such as these can then be followed by closed-ended questions. "Do you have palpitations?" "Shortness of breath?" "Is there heart disease in your family?" "What medications are you taking?" Such questions elicit short, specific answers that are useful for testing specific hypotheses.

Carefully address any clusters of symptoms described by the patient, and look for patterns. The presence of any of the symptoms listed in Table 1 should always raise the possibility of an anxiety state. If several of the symptoms in the first column occur in unexpected, unprovoked attacks, then the symptoms are characteristic and specific to panic disorder. Patients who are not anxious typically report few of these symptoms, and do not report them as occurring in clusters. If the patient has two or more symptoms from the table without physical cause, then an anxiety disorder is a strong possibility.

Inquire about the frequency and severity of each of the symptoms, and have the patient describe the most recent epi-

INTERVIEWING PRINCIPLES AND TECHNIQUES

- **Invest the time.** Take the time to get the whole story. Make a precise diagnosis, either during one scheduled comprehensive evaluation or through several visits that focus on different elements of the patient's disorder.

- **Structure the interview.** Provide adequate time for the patient to relate the story of the illness, and for you to elicit the complete agenda, negotiate priorities, and focus on priority issues.

- **Review a few issues during each visit.** Don't try to respond to all of the patient's symptoms, concerns, questions, and hypotheses in a single visit.

- **Use effective interview techniques.** Use open-ended questions, listen actively, summarize, and check (reaffirm).

- **Convey your willingness to listen** through eye contact, proper distance and posture, and empathic responses.

- **Negotiate an agenda for each session**— but be flexible and open to new issues. Keep your staged evaluation and interventions orderly and productive. Consider a written agreement for complex agendas.

- **Abide by time constraints** by terminating each session in a punctual manner. Carefully bring all important issues to a close by recapitulating the major points of each discussion.

- **Target the most important symptoms and keep accurate records.** Note the frequency, severity, and related disability of these symptoms. Good records facilitate successful therapy.

- **Review in detail your patient's use of nonpharmacologic interventions.** Review how, when, and with what effects the patient uses prescribed interventions. Look for successes and impediments. Negotiate solutions.

- **Educate the patient regularly.** Review important aspects of treatment and provide educational materials whenever possible.

sode or attack in detail, along with the circumstances under which they occurred. Also ask the patient about past emotional problems and major life stresses.

Patients may forget or suppress matters they had originally intended to discuss. Thus, it often helps to summarize the original complaint and then say, "Is there anything else you wish to talk about?" If time is limited, arrangements can be made to cover these matters at a subsequent visit.

The return visit is an opportunity to renew and strengthen the relationship begun earlier. Recapitulating your evaluation and any progress made at the previous visit will help the patient understand and accept the diagnosis, as well as appreciate the importance of all therapeutic interventions. Return visits are also important for surveying problems again, learning of significant changes between visits, and checking the effect of diagnostic and therapeutic interventions. Formal assessment tools (see Assessment Tools in the Appendix) can help the physician measure changes over time.

Step 3: Evaluate. Assess the patient's general mental status, paying particular attention to the following:

- *Appearance and behavior.* Although appearance and behavior can provide effective diagnostic clues, many patients with anxiety disorders do not appear anxious during the initial interview. For example, patients with generalized anxiety disorder may appear anxious, while patients with panic disorder may appear calm. Patients with posttraumatic stress disorder often appear emotionally labile and tense.

- *Mood and affect.* Fear or apprehension suggests anxiety; a dominant mood of sadness and loss of interest in usual activities points toward depression.

- *Speech.* The content and flow of the patient's speech can sometimes provide diagnostic clues. Psychomotor retardation suggests the presence of depression, while pressure of speech suggests mania.

- *Thought content.* Disruptions of thought content may occur in depression, as well as in obsessive-compulsive and psychotic disorders. Inquire about phobias, obsessions, compulsions, and excessive fears or bodily preoccupation.

SIX STEPS TO DIAGNOSING AN ANXIETY DISORDER

STEP 1: Listen
Listen to the patient's description of the pattern of complaints.

STEP 2: Inquire
If the pattern of complaints is consistent with an anxiety disorder, inquire about the presence of other common symptoms of anxiety. Look for clusters of symptoms.

STEP 3: Evaluate
Evaluate the patient's appearance and behavior, mood and affect, flow and content of speech, thought content and intellectual function, insight into illness, judgment, and degree of disability and social adjustment.

STEP 4: Examine
Do a physical examination to look for other disorders and identify concomitant medical problems. Also do any indicated laboratory tests.

STEP 5: Inform
If symptoms of anxiety are present, inform the patient of the possibility of an anxiety disorder and explore the patient's attributions and beliefs.

STEP 6: Clarify
Look for evidence of an associated disorder presenting with anxiety or of comorbidity (alcoholism, substance abuse, depression, etc.). Review all the facts and establish a specific diagnosis.

Suspect an anxiety disorder if the patient reports dysfunction in any of the following body systems: cardiac, pulmonary, gastrointestinal, or central or peripheral nervous system.

- *Intellectual function.* Inquire about orientation and memory. Disruption of intellectual function suggests the presence of an organic brain syndrome such as delirium. Intellectual function is intact in persons with anxiety disorders.

- *Insight into illness.* Patients with anxiety disorders are often reluctant to accept a psychological explanation for their physical condition.

- *Judgment.* Impaired judgment may signify an organic brain syndrome or a psychotic disorder.

- *Impairment and social adjustment.* Determining the patient's degree of impairment and social adjustment can provide important guidelines by which to evaluate and treat an anxiety disorder.

Step 4: Examine. Perform a tailored physical examination to look for other disorders, such as hyperthyroidism, that mimic anxiety disorders, as well as to identify concomitant diseases or medical problems. The physical examination reassures patients that their concerns are taken seriously. Perform laboratory tests indicated by the pattern of the patient's complaints and concerns, and the physical findings. Consider not only the concerns of the differential diagnosis, but also conditions such as alcoholism that can influence the choice of therapy.

Step 5: Inform. Explore the patient's attributions and preconceptions about the illness and about anxiety as a diagnostic possibility. Sometime during the first interview, if appropriate, inform the patient of the possibility of an anxiety disorder and begin to educate the patient about the new approach to anxiety outlined in this book. Patients who are prepared and who feel they are understood are more likely to be receptive to the final diagnosis and cooperate with treatment.

Step 6: Clarify. Explore the possibility of an associated disorder that can present with anxiety-related symptoms. Use direct questions to evaluate the possible coexistence of alcoholism or other substance abuse, depression, schizophrenia, and suicide risk. (Subsequent sections of Part One discuss these important medical problems, which may present with anxiety symptoms or coexist with anxiety disorders.) Finally, review all the information acquired during the interview and establish a specific diagnosis.

PSYCHOTIC ANXIETY

Intense anxiety or agitation is sometimes the major presenting symptom of an acute episode of schizophrenia or other psychotic disorder. This situation may be confusing, especially when it occurs in an individual without a previous history of a psychotic disorder. Major diagnostic features include thought disorganization, delusional thinking, paranoid ideation, thought insertion, marked fluctuations in affect and behavior, and "clang" or rhyme associations. ("Clanging" speech consists of disconnected ideas based on the sound of words rather than their meaning; it may include rhyming and punning.)

Anxiety can also be a predominant symptom in a patient who will gradually develop psychotic symptoms over time. In such cases, the diagnosis can be established only with follow-up observation.

When a diagnosis of psychotic anxiety is suspected, the patient should be seen promptly by a psychiatrist, mental health clinic, or hospital emergency staff.

DRUG-INDUCED ANXIETY

Many medications can produce, exacerbate, or mimic the physical or psychological symptoms of anxiety during use or withdrawal. Examples include thyroid medications in high doses, asthma preparations such as theophylline, and the sympathomimetics — especially anorexiants. High-dose corticosteroid therapy (50 mg or more of prednisone — sometimes less in rare cases) can also induce anxiety, as can corticosteroid withdrawal.

Because many drugs and drug classes have been implicated in anxiety states, a careful drug history is an important part of every anxiety evaluation.

References

1. Lipkin M Jr, Quill TE, Napodano RJ: The medical interview: A core curriculum for residencies in internal medicine. *Ann Intern Med* 1984;100:277-284.
2. Lipkin M Jr: Psychiatry and medicine, in Kaplan HI, Sadock BI (eds): *Comprehensive Textbook of Psychiatry*, ed 4. Baltimore, Williams & Wilkins Co, 1985.
3. Burnside JW, McGlynn TJ: Physician relationships and the patient interview, in *Physical Diagnosis*, ed 17. Baltimore, Williams & Wilkins, 1987, chap 2.
4. Beckman HB, Frankel RM: The effect of physician behavior on the collection of data. *Ann Intern Med* 1984;101:692-696.

The lifetime prevalence of alcohol abuse or dependence is approximately 24 percent for men and 4 to 5 percent for women.[1] It may be especially high in anxious patients because: (1) patients with anxiety disorders frequently self-medicate with alcohol, (2) recurrent anxiety is prevalent among substance and alcohol abusers, and (3) anxiety symptoms are common during alcohol withdrawal.

Screening for Alcohol Abuse

All patients who present with anxiety-related symptoms should be screened for alcohol abuse. The four questions that comprise the CAGE Questionnaire for Alcoholism (see the Appendix) provide an efficient, effective screen. The CAGE questions can be incorporated easily into the history-taking during the medical interview. A useful way to begin the discussion is to say something like "Most people take a drink occasionally. Do you?" Then work in the four CAGE questions.

If all of the responses are negative, the CAGE takes only a minute or two to administer. If any answers are positive, further questioning should be used to establish the patient's drinking patterns and the extent of the problem, and to identify other evidence of current or past alcohol-related problems.[2]

A family history of alcohol abuse is strongly associated with a higher risk of developing alcoholism. For example, a male with an alcoholic father has a 1 in 4 chance of also becoming an alcoholic.[3] A blood alcohol level of over 150 mg/dL in a patient without obvious signs of intoxication indicates alcohol tolerance and is usually diagnostic of alcoholism.[4]

Managing the Alcoholic Patient

Once the presence of alcoholism is established, the physician's approach should be nonjudgmental and nonargumentative, but firm and definite. Denial and, occasionally, cognitive dysfunction may limit the patient's ability to respond constructively to the diagnosis, but may not preclude proceeding with treatment. It is useful to emphasize that alcohol abuse is a biological disorder, not a failure of willpower or morality. Medical support in the form of a concrete treatment program maximizes the chances for recovery. Alcoholic patients who attempt to cut back on their own or are simply advised to do so without support or therapy have a low success rate.

The main goals of therapy are for the patient to regain both control (usually through long-term abstinence) and self-esteem. Some patients and families benefit from written information about the disorder. Arranging for a representative from a support group such as Alcoholics Anonymous to phone or meet with the patient is often helpful. Many patients will not enter a treatment program unless they are threatened with severe consequences, such as loss of family, job, or driving privileges. In general, the physician should be firm, supportive, and informative. Coercion should be used only when all else fails and the patient's life and family are seriously disrupted. Family members may be advised to join support groups to help them cope with and understand the alcoholic patient. Involvement of family members enhances significantly the overall outcome of therapeutic interventions.

Anxiolytics have a very limited role in the management of the alcoholic patient. The combination of benzodiazepines and alcohol can produce serious reactions including amnesia, profound stupor, respiratory depression, and cardiac arrest. In hospitalized patients with severe, acute withdrawal symptoms, beta blockers or benzodiazepines may be indicated in conjunction with close supervision to detect and manage any respiratory problems or other complications. In carefully selected outpatients who are willing to participate in a comprehensive rehabilitation program with frequent follow-up, cautious, short-term use of an anxiolytic or a trial of antidepressant medication may be appropriate if specifically indicated. Prescriptions should be written for the smallest number of pills feasible. Special caution should be used in patients with advanced alcoholic liver disease, as it may impair drug metabolism and elimination.

References

1. Robins LN, Helzer JE, Weissman MM, et al: Lifetime prevalence of specific psychiatric disorders in three sites. *Arch Gen Psychiatry* 1984;41:949-958.
2. Barnes HN, Aronson MD, Delbanco TL: *Alcoholism: A Guide for the Primary Care Physician.* New York, Springer-Verlag, 1987.
3. Goodwin DW: Studies of familial alcoholism: A review. *J Clin Psychiatry* 1984; 45:14-17.
4. Criteria Committee, National Council on Alcoholism: Criteria for the diagnosis of alcoholism. *Ann Intern Med* 1972; 77:249-258.

Table 1
Features Common to Both
Anxiety and Depression

- Sleep disturbances
- Appetite changes
- Nonspecific cardiopulmonary or gastrointestinal complaints
- Difficulty concentrating
- Irritability
- Fatigue, lack of energy

The distinction between anxiety and depression can be difficult. Studies have found a high incidence of anxious symptoms in patients with major depression, as well as a high incidence of depressive symptoms in patients with anxiety disorders.[1-4] To further complicate matters, a number of symptoms—including sleep and appetite disturbances, difficulty concentrating, irritability, and fatigue—can be characteristic of both anxiety and depression (see Table 1).

Careful diagnosis is the key to effective treatment and long-term management of anxiety and depressive disorders. In primary care practices, patients may present with a variety of nonspecific signs and symptoms that may not fit strict diagnostic criteria. Nevertheless, even when symptoms appear to be "mixed," every effort should be made to establish the primary diagnosis. The major distinguishing features of anxiety and depression are discussed below and summarized in Tables 2 and 3.

- **Predominant mood.** Depressed patients are typically sad, hopeless, joyless, "down in the dumps." Although they may also describe themselves as anxious, angry, worried, or tense, an underlying current of despair can usually be uncovered on close questioning. Anxious patients, on the other hand, are predominantly fearful—afraid of having another panic attack or of confronting the phobic stimulus.

- **Age of onset.** Panic disorder typically begins during the late teens or early 20s, with an average of 26 ± 6 years.[5,6] Onset after age 45 is exceedingly rare, although not impossible. In depression, the average age of onset is about 30, but the range is enormous—anywhere from 12 to 75.[7] Thus, if an older patient presents with worsening anxiety, a primary depressive disorder is a likely diagnosis.

  Since the other anxiety disorders are much less common than panic disorder, their distinction from depression is a less frequent problem. It may be helpful to note that obsessive-compulsive disorder and social phobia, like panic disorder, have, on average, early ages of onset—26 ± 14 years and 16 ± 8 years,[5,6] respectively.

- **Sleep patterns.** Insomnia can occur in either depressive or anxious states, but the typical patterns differ. Anxious patients are more likely to report difficulty

Table 2
Features More Characteristic of Anxiety

- Difficulty falling asleep ("initial" insomnia)
- Phobic avoidance behavior
- Rapid pulse and other evidence of psychomotor and autonomic hyperactivity
- Breathing disturbances
- Apprehensive expectation, feelings of dread
- Tremors, palpitations
- Sweating, hot or cold spells
- Faintness, light-headedness, dizziness
- Depersonalization (feelings of detachment from all or part of one's body)
- Derealization (a sensation that the immediate environment is strange, unreal, unfamiliar)

Table 3
Features More Characteristic of Depression

- Early-morning awakening ("late" insomnia) or hypersomnia
- Diurnal variation (feeling worse in the morning)
- Sad, downcast facial expression
- Slowed speech, slowed thought processes, delayed response time, reduced mobility of facial expression and body movement, and other evidence of psychomotor retardation (agitation may also occur)
- Chronic or recurrent nagging pain (not otherwise explainable)
- Feelings of sadness, guilt, hopelessness, worthlessness, despair
- Loss of interest in usual activities
- Anhedonia (loss of ability to experience pleasure)
- Difficulty making decisions
- Thoughts of death or suicide

in falling asleep ("initial" insomnia), whereas depressed patients typically report early-morning awakening and inability to get back to sleep ("late" insomnia). Excessive sleeping (hypersomnia) may also occur in depression.

- **Psychomotor signs.** Depressed patients often exhibit noticeable psychomotor retardation, with slowing of speech and increased response latency, but they may also appear agitated. Anxious patients may appear either fidgety or calm, but they rarely show signs of slowing.

- **Other symptoms.** Depressed patients are more likely to report difficulty making decisions and loss of interest in usual activities. Although somatic symptoms can be prominent in either depressive or anxious states, chronic pain tends to be more typical of depression.

- **Family history.** Patients with panic disorder often report similar symptoms in family members. Depressed patients are more likely to have family histories of depression or bipolar illness.

- **Substance use.** Alcohol use can accompany either depressive or anxiety disorders. Although anxious patients may be unusually suspicious of drugs and fearful of addiction, they may use alcohol in a conscious or unconscious attempt to treat their symptoms. According to some investigators, depressed patients are more likely than anxious patients to misuse prescribed drugs.[8] Depressed patients may lower their alcohol intake because of a decrease in socializing or raise their intake in an attempt to treat their insomnia or ease their psychic pain. In many cases, patients with anxiety or depression can identify precisely which drugs make them feel better or worse, and these reactions may provide diagnostic clues. For example, caffeine, amphetamines, and marijuana may exacerbate panic disorder or be mood lifters in depression. For more information on substance use and abuse, see Anxiety and Alcohol Abuse and Pharmacologic Treatment.

- **Response to exercise.** Moderately depressed patients may report that exercise makes them feel better temporarily; however, their interest in exercise is likely to vary as their moods vary. Severely depressed patients will find it difficult to impossible to exercise. Patients with panic disorder may report (quite physiologically) that exercise makes them feel worse.

- **Psychosocial effects.** Patients with panic disorder complicated by agoraphobia may be quite limited in their ability to engage in activities outside the home. Despite this, they frequently have supportive spouses and normal sex lives. In contrast, depressed patients are more likely to have difficulty in every psychosocial sphere. They may lose interest in sex and become irritable and withdrawn, impairing relationships with their spouses and children. Since they concentrate poorly, their work is often affected. And as they become less spontaneous and engaged, they tend to withdraw socially. Thus, the hallmark of depression is an across-the-board interference with life.

When diagnostic criteria are followed carefully, however, some patients do meet the conditions for both an anxiety disorder *and* major depression. In such cases, both disorders should be diagnosed and treatment should proceed accordingly. An antidepressant is often the drug of first choice.

Depression Secondary to Anxiety Disorders

When panic disorder or other anxiety disorders cause progressive disability and impairment of work, social, and family life, secondary depression can occur. Feelings of guilt and low self-esteem are common, as patients agonize over their inability to function normally; to shop, socialize, or travel; and to cope with the ordinary stresses of life. The severity of the depressed feelings is often closely related to the severity of the anxiety disorder. Secondary depression should be treated first, following the same protocol used for treating primary depression. The patient should then be observed for evidence of an underlying disorder, which should be treated.

Much diagnostic confusion has resulted from observing anxiety disorders and their complications at different stages of progression. A patient with panic disorder, for example, may move rapidly through several stages—limited symptom attacks, panic attacks, hypochondriasis, limited phobic avoidance, extensive phobic avoidance, secondary depression; remain for an extended period at one stage—limited symptom attacks; or alternately worsen and improve. In some patients, the stages may not follow the usual sequence (see Panic Disorder With or Without Agoraphobia in Part Two for more information).

Diagnostic errors have been made by assigning different labels to the predominant symptoms of different stages of the same disorder. In general, a long-range view and an understanding of the natural history of each disorder will result in the most accurate diagnosis.

Guidelines for Treatment

When patients present with symptoms of more than one disorder, treatment must often be initiated for the "best-fit diagnosis," targeted to the most prominent symptoms. The patient should then be observed closely, and the physician should be prepared to alter treatment if no improvement is seen in six to eight weeks. Secondary symptom clusters may improve spontaneously as the primary disorder improves. On the other hand, treatment may uncover an underlying primary disorder. For example, benzodiazepines may relieve the anxiety, but the depression emerges and the appropriate diagnosis of major depression becomes evident. Most depressed patients will not respond adequately to antianxiety therapy alone, so a tricyclic antidepressant should be given. Single-drug therapy is always preferred where possible.

When both anxiety and depression are present, treatment of depression takes precedence. A sedating tricyclic antidepressant is the drug of choice.

Over time, the patient's response to treatment may suggest revisions in the initial "working" diagnosis. Ultimately, diagnostic precision is the best foundation for choosing both pharmacologic and nonpharmacologic treatment, and for managing complications, relapses, and long-term follow-up.

For details on treatment of specific anxiety disorders, see Part Two.

References

1. Robins LN, Helzer JE, Weissman MM: Lifetime prevalence of specific psychiatric disorders in three sites. *Arch Gen Psychiatry* 1984;41:949-959.
2. Hamilton M: The clinical distinction between anxiety and depression. *Br J Clin Pharmacol* 1983;15(suppl 2):165-169.
3. Schurman RA, Kramer PD, Mitchell JB: The hidden mental health network: Treatment of mental illness by nonpsychiatrist physicians. *Arch Gen Psychiatry* 1985; 42:89-94.
4. Fawcett J, Kravitz HM: Anxiety syndromes and their relationship to depressive illness. *J Clin Psychiatry* 1983;44:8-11.
5. Thyer BA, Parrish RT, Curtis GC, et al: Ages of onset of DSM-III anxiety disorders. *Compr Psychiatry* 1985;26:113-122.
6. Reich J: The epidemiology of anxiety. *J Nerv Ment Dis* 1986;174:129-136.
7. Winokur G: Unipolar depression, in Winokur G, Clayton P (eds): *The Medical Basis of Psychiatry*. Philadelphia, WB Saunders, 1986.
8. Garvey MJ, Tollefson GD: Prevalence of misuse of prescribed benzodiazepines in patients with primary anxiety disorder or major depression. *Am J Psychiatry* 1986;143:1601-1603.

Patients who present with physical symptoms for which no organic or physiologic cause can be found are often labeled hypochondriacs and somatizers—or, at the other extreme, subjected to unnecessary and potentially dangerous tests, procedures, and medications. These patients warrant a thorough assessment; however, the assessment should be aimed at ruling *in* the most probable causes for this phenomenon, rather than making exhaustive attempts to rule out less likely possibilities first.

Although patients with anxiety and depressive disorders may focus exclusively on their physical symptoms, frequently denying any subjective experience of mental distress, the primary care physician should be alert to the possibility of symptom clusters suggesting such disorders as panic disorder, generalized anxiety disorder, or agitated or masked depression. Remember: *The absence of subjective mental distress or psychosocial stressors does not rule out the presence of an anxiety or depressive disorder*. These disorders can and do present both with and without subjective "emotional" symptoms. The physician who does not recognize the characteristic symptom clusters may overlook these definable and highly treatable disorders.

A thorough assessment should include an exploration of the patient's current life setting and personal relationships, as well as any history of vaguely defined medical ailments or illness behavior. Keep in mind that an underlying personality disorder or somatoform disorder may complicate the clinical presentation. The time spent in eliciting the patient's complaints or description of the symptoms and taking a complete medical and psychosocial history, rather than seeking the "quick fix" of a simple medical or psychosocial diagnosis, will be well spent.

The essential features of the somatoform disorders are physical symptoms for which there are no demonstrable organic findings or known physiologic mechanisms, and for which there is positive evidence or a strong presumption that the symptoms are linked to psychological factors or conflicts. Because nonspecific symptoms from several organ systems can be presenting features of both an anxiety and a somatoform disorder, an anxiety disorder sometimes may be misdiagnosed as a somatoform disorder, and vice versa. *The presence of a somatoform disorder, however, does not rule out the possibility of an anxiety disorder.*

The four major *DSM-III-R*[1] categories of somatoform disorders are hypochondriasis, somatization disorder, conversion disorder, and somatoform pain disorder. Because the first two—hypochondriasis and somatization disorder—are most likely to coexist with or obscure the diagnosis of an anxiety disorder (especially panic disorder), they are discussed in more detail below.

Hypochondriasis

Hypochondriasis is the fear of having, or the belief that one has, a serious disease (see the full diagnostic criteria in Table 1). Preoccupied with their bodies, hypochondriacal patients appear to have abnormal responses to normal sensations, or amplified responses to minor abnormal sensations.[2,3]

Hypochondriasis can be a symptom of an undiagnosed anxiety disorder such as panic disorder. In an effort to explain and to cope with physical symptoms, a patient with panic disorder can focus on the pos-

sibility of a severe underlying physical disorder. If panic disorder (or other primary mental disorder) is diagnosed and treated, the hypochondriacal symptoms often disappear.[4]

True hypochondriacs are often extremely distressed persons; their fears and preoccupations may disrupt social functioning and personal relationships. Such patients are often best managed by the primary care physician in consultation with a psychiatrist.

Somatization Disorder

Somatization disorder is also characterized by preoccupation with somatic complaints; however, patients focus more on specific *symptoms* rather than on fear of specific diseases as in hypochondriasis. Prevalence estimates range from 0.2 to 2 percent and are higher among women. Patients typically have a history of multiple physical complaints lasting several years, starting before age 30, carry multiple diagnoses, take many medications, and have many drug allergies. These patients repeatedly seek medical explanations for their physical symptoms and willingly undergo diagnostic procedures, surgeries, and clinical trials even though such efforts are rarely successful.[5-7] Their complaints usually involve conversion or pseudoneurologic symptoms, gastrointestinal discomfort, female reproductive difficulties, psychosexual problems, pain, and cardiopulmonary symptoms.[1] In addition, these patients have at least 13 of the symptoms (without organic or physiologic cause) listed in Table 2.[1] Somatization disorder is not diagnosed when the physical symptoms occur only during panic at-

Table 1
Diagnostic Criteria for Hypochondriasis

- Fear of having or the belief that one has a serious disease, based on the person's interpretation of physical signs or sensations as evidence of physical illness.

- Complaint of physical disorder is not supported by appropriate physical evaluation and the symptoms do not meet the criteria for panic attacks.

- Fear/belief of getting or having the disease persists regardless of medical reassurance.

- Disturbance duration of at least six months.

- The fear/belief is not of delusional intensity; the patient can acknowledge the possibility that it is unfounded.

Adapted with permission from *DSM-III-R*.[1]

Table 2
Diagnostic Criteria for Somatization Disorder

(Note that these complaints contrast sharply with those seen in anxiety disorders — see Table 1, "Symptoms of Anxiety" on page 2.)

Gastrointestinal symptoms:

- **vomiting (other than during pregnancy)**
- abdominal pain (other than when menstruating)
- nausea (other than motion sickness)
- bloating (gassy)
- diarrhea
- intolerance of (gets sick from) several different foods

Pain symptoms:

- **pain in extremities**
- back pain
- joint pain
- pain during urination
- other pain (excluding headaches)

Cardiopulmonary symptoms:

- **shortness of breath when not exerting oneself**
- palpitations
- chest pain
- dizziness

Conversion or pseudoneurologic symptoms:

- **amnesia**
- **difficulty swallowing**
- loss of voice

- deafness
- double vision
- blurred vision
- blindness
- fainting or loss of consciousness
- seizure or convulsion
- trouble walking
- paralysis or muscle weakness
- urinary retention or difficulty urinating

Sexual symptoms for the major part of the person's life after opportunities for sexual activity:

- **burning sensation in sexual organs or rectum other than during intercourse**
- sexual indifference
- pain during intercourse
- impotence

Female reproductive symptoms judged by the person to occur more frequently or severely than in most women:

- **painful menstruation**
- irregular menstrual periods
- excessive menstrual bleeding
- vomiting throughout pregnancy

Note: The seven items in boldface may be used to screen for the disorder. The presence of two or more of these items suggests a high likelihood of the disorder.

Reprinted with permission from *DSM-III-R*, pp 263-264.[1]

tacks. However, panic disorder and somatization disorder can coexist.

While there may be a spectrum of milder phenomena that mimic somatization disorder, patients who truly meet the criteria often have lives that are dominated by medical experiences and may have disturbed personal relationships. The family history often reveals similar illnesses in the women and antisocial behavior in the men.

When considering a diagnosis of somatization disorder, it is important to take a complete medical and psychosocial history, and to use medications and diagnostic tests conservatively. If the longstanding pattern of illness behavior is not truly present, then the possibility of another mental or physical disorder should be considered.

References

1. American Psychiatric Association: *Diagnostic and Statistical Manual of Mental Disorders*, Third Edition—Revised. Washington, DC, American Psychiatric Association, 1987.
2. Barsky AJ, Klerman GL: Overview: Hypochondriasis, bodily complaints, and somatic styles. *Am J Psychiatry* 1983; 140:273-283.
3. Barsky AJ III: Patients who amplify bodily sensations. *Ann Intern Med* 1979; 91:63-70.
4. Noyes R, Reich J, Clancy J, et al: Reduction in hypochondriasis with treatment of panic disorder. *Br J Psychiatry* 1986;149:631-635.
5. Kaplan C, Lipkin M, Gordon G: Somatization in primary care: Patients with unexplained and vexing complaints. *J Gen Intern Med* 1988;3:177-190.
6. Quill TE: Somatization disorder: One of medicine's blind spots. *JAMA* 1985; 254:3075-3079.
7. Ford CV: *Somatizing Disorders: Illness as a Way of Life*. New York, Elsevier Biomedical, 1983.

This Handbook focuses on recognizing and treating the anxiety disorders classified in the *DSM-III-R*.[1] These anxiety disorders are listed on Axis I of the *DSM-III-R* multiaxial evaluation system (see The Problem List for Classification). Some patients, however, have symptoms that seem to be an expression of their basic underlying personality. In such cases, recognizing and treating the anxiety disorders alone may not be enough.

Personality style is as stable and characteristic as eye color; that is, individuals tend to behave in recognizable patterns. Although each individual is unique, certain character traits are likely to occur in natural clusters; for example, highly conscientious persons are often orderly, meticulous, and (perhaps) excessively devoted to work.

A patient's personality is of concern to the physician when it either interferes with adherence to the medical regimen or contributes to the patient's symptoms. During serious medical illness, patients often react and behave more immaturely than usual, and their personality features tend to become more prominent and more rigid. Although this can cause difficulties for the treating physician, there are well-established ways of recognizing and contending with the impact of the patient's personality on medical treatment.[2]

Some individuals, however, have chronically maladaptive personality styles that persist during periods of health or illness. In psychiatric terms, these individuals are said to have a "personality disorder."[3] Specific personality disorder diagnoses, as well as prominent personality factors, are recorded on Axis II of the multiaxial system.

Personality disorders can and usually do coexist with Axis I diagnoses, including the anxiety disorders. The physician who treats an Axis I disorder without addressing prominent Axis II features or disorders is likely to find that the treatment efforts fail. The literature suggests that the presence of a personality disorder in association with an anxiety disorder worsens treatment response and outcome.[4] In some cases, a personality disorder is actually the primary source of the patient's difficulties.

A comprehensive discussion of personality disorders is beyond the scope of this Handbook; however, the subject is of importance in this context for two reasons: (1) anxiety is often a prominent feature of a personality disorder and (2) many patients with anxiety disorders have personality factors that complicate or impede treatment. A brief discussion of selected personality disorders follows. Avoidant, dependent, obsessive-compulsive, passive-aggressive, and borderline personality disorders are emphasized here, since they often present with anxiety as a prominent feature. For a full listing of the criteria for each diagnosis, refer to the *DSM-III-R*.

Avoidant personality disorder. Persons with avoidant personality disorder want to

---

MANAGING PATIENTS WITH PERSONALITY PROBLEMS

The following guidelines can aid the primary care physician in treating anxious patients who have complicating personality factors or disorders:

- Observe personality style during assessment of any anxious patient, adapting within reasonable limits to the patient's preferred modes of interaction.

- Consider the possibility of a personality disorder as a complicating factor, especially when treatment fails to produce the expected response.

- Revise your expectations regarding treatment outcome if one or more personality disorder diagnoses apply. Patients with personality disorders typically have poorer responses to treatment for anxiety disorders and other psychiatric or medical diagnoses.

- Treat any Axis I syndromes vigorously. *Many symptoms and characteristics that appear to be personality problems will improve or disappear with proper treatment of the Axis I disorder(s).*

- Consider psychiatric consultation or referral, if indicated.

interact with others and have the capacity to do so, but they deal with their social anxiety by avoidance. They are hypersensitive to rejection, fear embarrassment, desire uncritical acceptance, and have exaggerated concerns about potential danger or discomfort in everyday situations. They are likely to have Axis I diagnoses related to phobias and anxiety.

Dependent personality disorder. Persons with dependent personality disorder rely excessively on others for support. They have difficulty taking initiative and feel helpless on their own. To avoid abandonment, they often stay in unproductive or unhappy social or work relationships, and they remain subordinate because they are afraid of functioning independently. They may be at risk for generalized anxiety disorder.

Obsessive-compulsive personality disorder. Persons with obsessive-compulsive personality disorder are perfectionists; their rigidity and perfectionism are pronounced enough to interfere with their effectiveness. Although their high standards may sometimes serve them well in their work, their inability to make decisions or to let go of tasks can be detrimental. Their controlling and demanding qualities often make their personal relationships unsatisfying. They may be at greater risk of developing obsessive-compulsive disorder, which is characterized by persistent intrusive thoughts and driven, ritualized behaviors.

Passive-aggressive personality disorder. Persons with passive-aggressive personality disorder express their aggression indirectly. Fearful of being criticized or rejected if they are assertive, they resist demands by procrastinating, "forgetting," or displaying deliberate indifference to tasks they don't like. Much or all of their behavior may be unconscious, and they typically do not acknowledge awareness of or responsibility for their exasperating ways. They often lack confidence and self-esteem and, in many cases, have never been valued for their intrinsic worth as human beings. To qualify for the diagnosis, the characteristic behavior must be pervasive, not simply situation-dependent.

Borderline personality disorder. Persons with borderline personality disorder can be difficult and demanding, with a persistent pattern of instability in their emotional and work lives. Their relationships often seesaw between extremes of idealizing and devaluing others, and they may have stormy relationships with their physicians. They are usually impulsive and have self-destructive habits such as excessive spending, substance abuse, indiscriminate sex, or binge-eating. They experience marked mood shifts, which are sudden, short-lived, and intense.

Anger is a prominent feature, with frequent displays of temper. Suicidal gestures, threats, and attempts, or self-mutilating behavior may be recurrent. Further, these patients have marked and persistent identity disturbance, shown by uncertainty about such basics as career choice, sexual orientation, values, and self-image. They feel chronically empty and bored, and they flee from those feelings, which they consider unbearable. Although they fear abandonment, they often precipitate it by their disturbed behavior. Not surprisingly, borderline patients often have acute and chronic anxiety and affective disorders, possibly complicated by substance abuse. The psychiatric literature on borderline patients is substantial and complicated; the interested reader can consult a classic clinical description,[5] current concepts of diagnosis,[6,7] and a recent summary of treatment approaches.[8]

References

1. American Psychiatric Association: *Diagnostic and Statistical Manual of Mental Disorders*, Third Edition—Revised. Washington, DC, American Psychiatric Association, 1987.
2. Kahana RJ, Bibring GL: Personality types in medical management, in Zinberg NE (ed): *Psychiatry and Medical Practice in a General Hospital.* New York, International Universities Press, 1965, pp 108-123.
3. Hirschfeld RMA (ed): Personality disorders, in Frances AJ, Hales RE (eds): *Psychiatry Update: American Psychiatric Association Annual Review*, vol 5. Washington, DC, American Psychiatric Press, 1986, pp 233-400.
4. Docherty JP, Fiester SJ, Shea T: Syndrome diagnosis and personality disorder, in Frances AJ, Hales RE (eds): *Psychiatry Update: American Psychiatric Association Annual Review*, vol 5. Washington, DC, American Psychiatric Press, 1986, pp 315-355.
5. Zetzel ER: The borderline patient. *Am J Psychiatry* 1971;127:43-47.
6. Gunderson JG, Singer MT: Defining borderline patients: An overview. *Am J Psychiatry* 1975;132:1-10.
7. Groves JE: Borderline personality disorder. *N Engl J Med* 1981;305:259-262.
8. Gelenberg AJ: Introduction: The borderline patient. *J Clin Psychiatry* 1987;48 (suppl):3-4.

Anxiety symptoms are present in many physical and mental disorders, as well as in common everyday social and interpersonal situations. This section briefly describes the seven major disorders of which anxiety is the primary component.

THE ANXIETY DISORDERS

The following criteria for anxiety disorders have been adapted for primary care from those in the *Diagnostic and Statistical Manual of Mental Disorders,* Third Edition—Revised (*DSM III-R*),[1] published in 1987 by the American Psychiatric Association. Widely used as psychiatry's current classification system, the *DSM-III-R* is the latest in an ongoing series of diagnostic classifications. The primary care physician often may justifiably decide to classify the anxious patient's symptomatology and begin treatment, rather than wait for the criteria to be met.

Panic Disorder With or Without Agoraphobia*

The characteristic feature of panic disorder is the presence of panic attacks, which are discrete periods (one to 60 minutes in duration) of intense fear or discomfort that are unexpected and not triggered by situations in which the person is the focus of others' attention.

To qualify for the diagnosis, patients must have either four attacks in a four-week period, or one or more attacks must have been followed by at least a month of persistent fear of having another attack. Further, at least four of the following symptoms must have developed during at least one of the attacks (the occurrence of fewer than four of the symptoms without any other obvious organic cause constitutes a "limited symptom" attack):

- shortness of breath (dyspnea) or smothering sensations
- dizziness, unsteady feelings, or faintness
- palpitations or accelerated heart rate
- trembling or shaking
- sweating
- choking
- nausea or abdominal distress
- depersonalization or derealization

---

*Paroxysmal anxiety disorder, ICD-10 draft, 1987

- numbness or tingling sensations
- hot flashes or chills
- chest pain or discomfort
- fear of dying
- fear of going crazy or of doing something uncontrolled.

The typical pattern is for the attacks to develop suddenly and to increase rapidly in intensity. For the diagnosis to be made, no organic factor (e.g., amphetamine or caffeine intoxication) can have initiated or maintained the disturbance. Most patients with panic disorder develop agoraphobia, which is the fear of being in places or situations from which escape might be difficult or embarrassing, or in which help might not be available if a panic attack occurred. As a result, patients either restrict travel or need a companion while away from home, or endure the agoraphobic situations despite the severe anxiety. Common agoraphobic situations include being outside the home alone; traveling in a bus, train, or car; crossing a bridge; or being in an elevator. For more information, see Panic Disorder With or Without Agoraphobia in Part Two.

Adjustment Disorder With Anxious Mood

An adjustment disorder is a *maladaptive reaction* to one or more identifiable psychosocial stressors that *occurs within three months* of onset of the stressor(s). The disturbance is not merely one instance of a pattern of overreaction to stress, nor is it an exacerbation of another mental disorder. For this diagnosis, the maladaptive reaction must persist for *no longer than six months* and the disturbance *must not meet the criteria for any other mental disorder* or for a normal but painful upset such as normal bereavement.

When the patient's predominant symptoms are nervousness, worry, and jitteriness, then the diagnosis is adjustment disorder with anxious mood. When the predominant manifestation is a combination of depression and anxiety or other emotions, then the diagnosis is adjustment disorder with mixed emotional features.

Many patients presenting with symptoms of anxiety in primary care settings will likely qualify for a diagnosis of adjustment disorder. For more information, see Adjustment Disorder With Anxious Mood in Part Two.

Table 1
Symptoms of Generalized Anxiety Disorder

Motor tension
- trembling, twitching, or feeling shaky
- muscle tension, aches, or soreness
- restlessness
- easy fatigability

Autonomic hyperactivity
- shortness of breath or smothering sensations
- palpitations or accelerated heart rate
- sweating, or cold clammy hands
- dry mouth
- dizziness or light-headedness
- nausea, diarrhea, or other abdominal distress
- flushes (hot flashes) or chills
- frequent urination
- trouble swallowing or "lump in throat"

Vigilance and scanning
- feeling keyed up or on edge
- exaggerated startle response
- difficulty concentrating or "mind going blank" because of anxiety
- trouble falling or staying asleep
- irritability

Adapted with permission from *DSM-III-R*.[1]

Obsessive-Compulsive Disorder

Obsessive-compulsive disorder can be distinguished by the presence of two elements: obsessions and compulsions. Obsessions are recurrent and persistent ideas, thoughts, impulses, or images that are intrusive, unwelcome, unwarranted, and repugnant. Examples include a parent's repeated impulses to sexually abuse a beloved child or a religious person's having recurrent blasphemous thoughts. The person tries to ignore or suppress such thoughts or impulses, or to neutralize them with some other thought or action. Further, he or she recognizes that the obsessions come from within the mind and are not imposed from without. Obsessions typically evoke anxiety, which leads to compulsions.

Compulsions are repetitive, purposeful, and intentional behaviors that a person performs in response to an obsession, or according to certain rules or in a stereotyped manner. The person considers that the behavior will neutralize or prevent discomfort or some dreaded event or situation. However, either the activity does not realistically relate to the dreaded results, or it is clearly excessive. Usually the person recognizes that the behavior is excessive or unreasonable. Afflicted persons have obsessions, compulsions, or both.

The obsessions or compulsions cause marked distress and consume more than an hour a day. Additionally, they interfere significantly with normal routine, occupational function, social activities, or interpersonal relationships. For more information, see Obsessive-Compulsive Disorder in Part Two.

Generalized Anxiety Disorder

Five clinical criteria must be met to make a diagnosis of generalized anxiety disorder. The first is unrealistic or excessive anxiety and worry (apprehensive expectation) about two or more life circumstances. *This worried mood occurs for a period of six months or longer*, during which time the person has been bothered more days than not by these concerns. Examples are worry about possible illness (without symptoms of the illness) or about finances (for no good reason).

Second, if another psychiatric diagnosis is present, the focus of the person's anxiety and worry is not in relation to that diagnosis.

Third, the disturbance does not occur with a mood or a psychotic disorder.

Fourth, the affected person suffers symptoms that can be clustered into three groups: motor tension, autonomic hyperactivity, and vigilance and scanning. For the diagnosis to apply, at least six of the 18 symptoms listed in Table 1 must be present when the person is anxious.

Finally, it cannot be established that an organic factor such as hyperthyroidism or caffeine intoxication initiated or maintained the symptoms. For more information, see Generalized Anxiety Disorder in Part Two.

Social Phobia

The characteristic feature of this disorder is a persistent fear of one or more situations in which a person feels subject to scrutiny and fears that he or she will do something humiliating or embarrassing. Common examples include the fear of being observed while eating, being unable to urinate in a public lavatory, and being unable to give a speech or perform in public, commonly known as "stage fright." Exposure to the specific phobic stimulus almost always provokes an immediate anxiety response. The person recognizes that the fear is excessive or unreasonable. *To make this diagnosis, the avoidant behavior must interfere significantly with occupational functioning or with social activities or interpersonal relationships.* For more information, see Social Phobia in Part Two.

Simple Phobia

Simple phobia is a persistent fear of an object, such as a dog or a cat, or a situation, such as flying, other than fear of having a panic attack (as in panic disorder) or of humiliation or embarrassment in certain social situations (as in social phobia). Exposure to the phobic stimulus almost always provokes anxiety immediately; the person either avoids such stimuli or endures the anxiety with great discomfort. Notably upset about having the fear, the patient recognizes it as excessive or unreasonable. *To make this diagnosis, the phobia must interfere significantly with the person's normal routine and social relationships.* For more information, see Simple Phobia in Part Two.

Posttraumatic Stress Disorder

In cases of posttraumatic stress, persons have experienced traumatic events that are outside the range of usual human experience and that almost anyone would find deeply upsetting. Examples include serious threat to the life or physical integrity of oneself, or one's children, spouse, or other loved ones (such as an accident, assault, rape, kidnapping, combat); sudden destruction of one's home or community; or being involved with someone who has been killed or seriously injured. Such persons exhibit at least one symptom indicating persistent reexperiencing of the trauma and display at least three symptoms of persistent avoidance of stimuli associated with the trauma. In addition, they have at least two persistent symptoms of increased arousal since the trauma and have experienced these symptoms for at least one month. For more information, see Posttraumatic Stress Disorder in Part Two.

THE PROBLEM LIST FOR CLASSIFICATION

As a general rule in medical practice, it is important to consider any presenting diagnosis in the larger context of the patient as a whole. The *DSM-III-R*[1] system of diagnosing anxiety and other mental disorders encourages the clinician to make a *comprehensive* diagnosis, using five axes to identify essential elements of the patient's clinical profile.

Axis I. The Axis I diagnoses consist of defined clinical symptom complexes, including the anxiety disorders that comprise the principal focus of this Handbook. A patient may meet the criteria for more than one Axis I diagnosis; thus, multiple diagnoses may apply. However, one primary diagnosis can usually be identified as the chief explanation for the patient's symptoms and the principal focus of treatment.

Axis II. This axis identifies prominent features of the patient's personality. Specified clusters of persistently maladaptive personality features are defined as personality *disorders*; in some cases, these disorders should be the primary focus of treatment. Prominent personality *trends* that fail to meet full criteria for a personality disorder may also need to be addressed in the treatment program (see Personality Factors and Personality Disorders).

Axis III. This axis is used to record any coexisting medical diagnoses; for example, diabetes mellitus.

Axis IV. This axis rates the severity of psychosocial stressors that have burdened the patient in the year preceding the current evaluation. Code numbers range from

1 (no significant stress), through 3 (moderate stress, e.g., marital separation), to 6 (catastrophic stress, e.g., death of a child).

Axis V. The last axis records a global assessment of function (GAF) on a scale of 1 to 90, based on psvchological, social, and occupational variables. Higher numbers indicate better function. For example, a patient who has many panic attacks with agoraphobia, drinks heavily, and is alienating his family and avoiding his friends has major impediments in several areas and would be given a GAF score of 35.

Modifying the DSM-III-R Classification System for Primary Care

The *DSM-III-R* psychiatric classification system lists diagnoses in a manner that identifies the total context of the patient's problem. Primary care physicians can modify the *DSM-III-R* system by using subcategories to identify key information about a patient's illness, such as functional severity and coexisting body system disorders.

Figure 1 demonstrates the use of this approach in classifying a patient who has diabetes mellitus with neuropathy and Class 2 coronary heart disease. The patient also has panic disorder and is undergoing a divorce. He is abusing alcohol, has passive-aggressive personality features, and is moderately impaired.

Reference

1. American Psychiatric Association: *Diagnostic and Statistical Manual of Mental Disorders*, Third Edition—Revised. Washington, DC, American Psychiatric Association, 1987.

Figure 1
Model Problem List

Primary Care	Psychiatry	
Coronary heart disease NYHA Class 2	Axis I:	Panic disorder with agoraphobia
		Alcohol abuse
Diabetes mellitus Neuropathy	Axis II:	Passive-aggressive personality features
Alcohol abuse	Axis III:	Coronary heart disease Diabetes mellitus with neuropathy
Panic disorder with agoraphobia Passive-aggressive personality features Stressors-Divorce (3) GAF-moderate impairment (60)	Axis IV:	Divorce (3)
	Axis V:	GAF 60

Recent surveys show that between 15 and 35 percent of patients who see primary care physicians have mental disorders; of these, at least one-third have some form of anxiety disorder.[1] Although primary care physicians usually recognize mental disturbances, they tend to classify them in general categories, such as unspecified depression, unspecified anxiety or "nervousness," and adjustment disorder, rather than assigning specific diagnoses.[2]

For an accurate diagnosis, which is essential to effective treatment, the physician must not only differentiate between the various anxiety disorders, but must also be aware of their prevalence in the general population. Epidemiologic data aid in diagnosis and suggest which individuals may be at greatest risk. The following discussion emphasizes epidemiologic information of greatest interest to primary care physicians.

The Epidemiologic Catchment Area Survey

The most extensive current data on the prevalence of anxiety disorders were collected during the Epidemiologic Catchment Area (ECA) survey of more than 9,000 adults living in three communities, conducted between 1980 and 1982 under the auspices of the National Institute of Mental Health.[3-5] This study used the criteria from the third edition of the *Diagnostic and Statistical Manual of Mental Disorders (DSM-III)*.[6] Generalized anxiety disorder, posttraumatic stress disorder, and adjustment disorder with anxious mood were not included in the survey.

Six-month prevalence. Figure 1 summarizes the ECA survey findings for six-month prevalence of selected disorders (i.e., for the six-month period immediately preceding the interview), by sex.[4] The prevalence of selected anxiety disorders is compared with that of alcohol abuse/dependence and affective disorders. Highlights of the findings are as follows:

- Anxiety disorders were found to be more than twice as common in women as in men.

- Prevalence rates for most mental disorders dropped sharply after age 45.

- Simple phobias were very common; however, the majority of simple phobias are circumscribed and do not cause significant subjective distress or disability.

- The prevalence of anxiety disorders (excluding simple phobia) in both men and women was about equal to that of the affective disorders.

Figure 1
Approximate Six-Month Prevalence of Selected Mental Disorders (%)

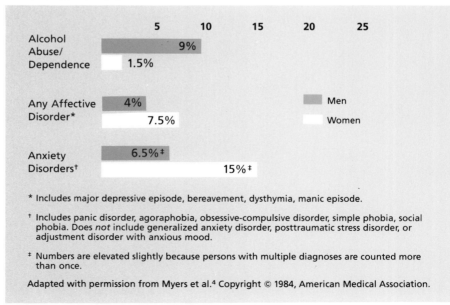

* Includes major depressive episode, bereavement, dysthymia, manic episode.

† Includes panic disorder, agoraphobia, obsessive-compulsive disorder, simple phobia, social phobia. Does *not* include generalized anxiety disorder, posttraumatic stress disorder, or adjustment disorder with anxious mood.

‡ Numbers are elevated slightly because persons with multiple diagnoses are counted more than once.

Adapted with permission from Myers et al.[4] Copyright © 1984, American Medical Association.

- In men, the prevalence of alcohol abuse/dependence exceeded that of both the anxiety and the affective disorders, and was six times greater than in women.

- Obsessive-compulsive disorder was about equally prevalent in women and men.

When the data are regrouped according to current *DSM-III-R*[7] criteria, the most common serious anxiety disorder becomes panic disorder, with or without agoraphobia.

Lifetime prevalence. The ECA survey also assessed the lifetime prevalence of selected anxiety disorders (i.e., the proportion of persons who had *ever* met the criteria for each disorder), as summarized in Figure 2.[5] The analysis revealed that:

- Anxiety disorders were again more than twice as common in women as in men.

- Alcohol abuse/dependence was five times more common in men than in women, affecting nearly one in four men.

- No outstanding differences in the prevalence of anxiety disorders could be seen on the basis of race, income, education, or rural versus urban dwelling.

For more information on the prevalence of specific anxiety disorders, see Part Two.

References

1. Kessler LG, Cleary PD, Burke JD Jr: Psychiatric disorders in primary care: Results of a follow-up study. *Arch Gen Psychiatry* 1985;42:583-587.
2. Von Korff M, Shapiro S, Burke JD, et al: Anxiety and depression in a primary care clinic. *Arch Gen Psychiatry* 1987;44: 152-156.
3. Regier DA, Myers JK, Kramer M, et al: The NIMH Epidemiologic Catchment Area program: Historical context, major objectives, and study population characteristics. *Arch Gen Psychiatry* 1984; 41:934-941.
4. Myers JK, Weissman MM, Tischler GL, et al: Six-month prevalence of psychiatric disorders in three communities: 1980 to 1982. *Arch Gen Psychiatry* 1984;41:959-967.
5. Robins LN, Helzer JE, Weissman MM, et al: Lifetime prevalence of specific psychiatric disorders in three sites. *Arch Gen Psychiatry* 1984;41:949-958.
6. American Psychiatric Association: *Diagnostic and Statistical Manual of Mental Disorders*, Third Edition. Washington, DC, American Psychiatric Association, 1980.
7. American Psychiatric Association: *Diagnostic and Statistical Manual of Mental Disorder*, Third Edition—Revised. Washington, DC, American Psychiatric Association, 1987.

Figure 2
Approximate Lifetime Prevalence of Selected Mental Disorders (%)

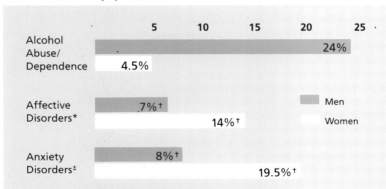

* Includes major depressive episode, dysthymia, manic episode.

† Numbers are elevated slightly because persons with multiple diagnoses are counted more than once.

‡ Includes panic disorder, agoraphobia, obsessive-compulsive disorder, simple phobia. Does *not* include social phobia, generalized anxiety disorder, posttraumatic stress disorder, or adjustment disorder with anxious mood.

Adapted with permission from Robins et al.[5] Copyright © 1984, American Medical Association.

In the past, anxiety disorders were usually held to be stress-related. Situational stressors and/or psychological conflicts were believed to be the sole etiologic factors. It was axiomatic that the greater the stress, the more severe the anxiety disorder. Thus, the focus of treatment was on resolving any apparent stress or conflict.

During the past decade, the focus has changed. Not all anxiety disorders fit the historical mold; strong evidence shows that some anxiety disorders are primarily biological illnesses associated with an underlying genetic vulnerability. Abnormalities associated with the GABA (gamma-aminobutyric acid)/benzodiazepine receptor complex, part of the major inhibitory neurotransmitter system in the brain, are believed to play an important role. GABA opens up ion channels in neuronal membranes, causing hyperpolarization of the neurons and decreasing their excitability—which results in a decrease in anxiety.

Research has also targeted the locus ceruleus in the brain, where stimulation elicits subjective feelings of anxiety. These and other proposed biological models of anxiety have stimulated research and may help develop more precise biological markers, laboratory tests, and treatment.

Anxiety that has a strong biological component responds poorly to psychological measures alone; it may respond well to pharmacologic treatment. Is stress, then, an unimportant etiologic factor? In some anxiety disorders—notably panic disorder and obsessive-compulsive disorder—stress may be much less central than once thought. Although stress and conflict can aggravate *any* illness, they are neither necessary nor sufficient to *cause* a biologically based anxiety disorder. But stress can make existing matters worse, and it should be explored and addressed in the treatment plan, whenever appropriate.

An Interplay of Forces

Usually, an interplay of three major forces—biological, psychosocial, and behavioral, corresponding to three proposed models—determines the nature and severity of an anxiety disorder. According to the *biological* model, anxiety disorders are genetically influenced physiologic diseases. The *psychosocial* model focuses on stresses and conflicts. And the *behavioral* model emphasizes conditioned responses that lead to acquisition of symptoms in accordance with classical learning theory.

Each causal model identifies a different dimension, but no one model is the whole story. In some anxiety disorders (e.g., simple phobia, adjustment disorder with anxious mood), the psychosocial and behavioral dimensions may predominate. In others (e.g., panic disorder), a biological predisposition may be critical. An *integrated* model is often best, accommodating all dimensions.

In panic disorder, for example, a genetic vulnerability may be a necessary precondition, and stress can be a switch that "turns on" the symptomatic expression of the underlying vulnerability. As the biological core is magnified, it facilitates the acquisition of phobias. As both of these factors intensify, they add stress to the patient's life. Any additional independent stress will further magnify the biological core and reinforce the phobic conditioning.

The relative contribution of each dimension may vary considerably from patient to patient. In general, the greater the genetic loading, the less stress is necessary to activate an anxiety disorder or produce a given degree of severity.

The central message for the physician is this: Don't limit your interpretation of your anxious patient's symptoms to a model based only on your own personal experience with anxiety. A model that is exclusively psychological or exclusively biological may be very misleading in attempting to understand and treat anxiety disorders. For additional details on the etiology of specific anxiety disorders, see Part Two.

Suggested Reading

Gray JA: *The Neuropsychology of Anxiety: An Inquiry into the Functions of the Septo-hippocampal System.* Oxford, Oxford University Press, 1982.

Insel TR, Ninan PT, Aloy J, et al: A benzodiazepine receptor mediated model of anxiety: Studies in non-human primates and clinical implications. *Arch Gen Psychiatry* 1984;41:741-750.

Redmond DE: Alterations in the function of the nucleus locus coeruleus: A possible model of four studies of anxiety. In Hanin I, Usdin E (eds): *Animal Models in Psychiatry and Neurology.* New York, Pergamon Press, 1977.

Reiman EM, Raichle ME, Butler FK, et al: PET focal brain abnormality in panic disorder. *Nature* 1984;310:683-685.

A variety of nonpharmacologic therapies are available to the physician in caring for the anxious patient. Educational, psychotherapeutic, behavioral, cognitive, social, and adjunctive approaches will be discussed here.

EDUCATIONAL APPROACHES

Educational approaches are especially important for patients with anxiety disorders. Early in treatment the physician should explain the disorder to the patient and provide steps the patient can take to control symptoms. This improves the patient's collaboration with the physician and encourages adherence to the treatment program. It is helpful for patients to know that their symptoms fit recognized patterns, that (often, but not always) many others share their symptoms, and that available treatment techniques (almost) always provide relief. Patients find it reassuring that the physician understands them, explains their symptoms, and provides them with varied ways of managing, easing, or doing away with their distress. Education validates the disease for the patient; that in itself is therapeutic. The physician's labeling of the patient's symptoms acknowledges to the patient that something is wrong. Such labeling is especially supportive to patients who have anxiety disorders, since anxiety symptoms are often vague.

The physician should review the patient's lifestyle and recommend practices that mediate life stresses. Recommendations that benefit all patients, especially those who are anxious, include sensible eating and drinking, adequate exercise, and proper rest. While simple to prescribe, these measures are often difficult to implement. A review of the patient's diet, and use of the CAGE Questionnaire for Alcoholism (see the Appendix), can be helpful. Excessive drinking commonly contributes to emotional upset and social dysfunction, but often goes unnoticed. In the physically dependent alcoholic, however, cessation of drinking can produce a prolonged withdrawal syndrome with associated anxiety. Caffeine in coffee or soft drinks worsens anxiety (and precipitates panic attacks), as does the nicotine in cigarettes.

PSYCHOTHERAPY

While many primary care physicians feel that "psychotherapy" is outside the scope of their practices, they commonly consider "counseling" an appropriate medical activity. Although many physicians underestimate its importance, the physician-patient relationship is in itself a powerful treatment tool. Kindly interest, attentive listening, persistent encouragement, and continued availability are the principal psychotherapeutic aspects of the physician's role. The physician's expressions of empathy—the capacity to "feel with" the patient—and unconditional positive regard for the patient, as well as helping patients identify and express their feelings, are all part of the supportive therapeutic relationship.

The physician should deal with patients directly, tactfully, and honestly, rather than relying on false reassurance, such as "It's going to be all right." Such statements may increase rather than ease a patient's distress. The psychotherapeutic benefits of even brief encounters can be achieved by encouraging the patient to talk and then by actively listening. The physician can build on the strong positive regard that patients usually have for physicians. This makes the doctor's recommendations and suggestions more powerful than those of friends, relatives, or colleagues.[1] Patients also benefit from the healing power of touch provided by the primary care physician in the conduct of the physical examination. The physician's touch supplements the physician's interest in and concern for the anxious patient.

Physicians with special interest and aptitude may want to learn more about psychotherapeutic approaches, to improve their effectiveness and to be able to refer knowledgeably.

Psychodynamic psychotherapy explores the bases of human behavior, to enable patients to gain insight into problems and change behavior. Psychodynamic principles and techniques work effectively in crisis intervention,[2] short- and long-term treatment,[3] and in couples, group, family, and individual therapy.

Dynamically oriented treatment is often available at community clinics, mental health centers, and university medical centers, as well as from private physicians.

BEHAVIOR THERAPY

Derived from learning theory, behavior therapy is aimed at changing specific behaviors in a structured, task-oriented, and usually short-term approach.[4] Behavior therapy may succeed in cases where psychodynamic approaches fail.[5] This is especially true when the symptom pattern is discrete, as in many phobias[6] and obsessive-compulsive disorder. In many cases, behavioral and psychodynamic approaches complement each other.

Behavior therapy begins with a formal evaluation, the functional assessment of behavior, that defines the parameters of the presenting problem, allowing the clinician to select appropriate treatment techniques. Behavioral techniques are diverse; the common principle in treating anxiety or phobias is direct *in vivo* exposure to the feared stimulus.

Systematic desensitization is a prominent behavioral treatment approach to anxiety symptoms. In this technique, the patient and the therapist construct a scale of scenes relating to the symptoms, ranking them in a hierarchy from least to most distressing. Using progressive muscular relaxation techniques, the patient learns to be relaxed while contemplating increasingly upsetting scenes in the hierarchy. Sessions move from the office to confronting anxiety-arousing situations in real life. Other behavioral approaches immerse the patient in the anxiety-provoking situation.

COGNITIVE THERAPY

Newest of the psychological approaches to symptom relief, cognitive therapy is based on the theory that a patient's distress results largely from distorted and inaccurate patterns of cognition, or thinking. In highly structured and specific approaches, cognitive therapy helps patients recast their maladaptive views of the world and take a more positive approach. Definitive research has not been done on the effectiveness of this treatment approach for the anxiety disorders; there is some evidence, however, that it is helpful in treating performance anxiety and social phobia.[7]

SOCIAL INTERVENTIONS

In recent years, physicians and mental health professionals alike have acknowledged the importance of the patient's social system in initiating and maintaining symptoms such as anxiety. Primary care physicians in general, and family physicians in particular, have more fully included the patient's social system, i.e., the family (biologic or otherwise), in the treatment program. Working with the family as a system has significant clinical advantages: it sharpens the diagnosis, speeds treatment, and improves patient compliance.[8] The physician can help by teaching the family about the anxiety disorder, encouraging relatives to acknowledge and tolerate their own mixed feelings about the patient's troubles and, when necessary, securing treatment for relatives as well as the identified patient.[9] The physician can support the family in the context of ongoing medical care.

ADJUNCTIVE TECHNIQUES

The primary care physician may recommend adjunctive techniques in treating the anxious patient. While each may be individually useful, none is a cure-all. The techniques are nonintrusive and can be part of a comprehensive treatment program. In addition, they provide patients with a broader range of treatment options.

Although some patients respond well to these adjunctive techniques, others have no response, and a small percentage have a negative reaction such as increased anxiety and psychological distress. Failure to respond or a negative reaction should prompt reassessment and possible referral for more specific psychological treatments. A brief description of several adjunctive techniques follows; consult the references at the end of this section for further information.

The relaxation response. The relaxation response is derived from the study of meditation techniques.[10] The patient sits quietly in a restful environment with eyes closed for 15 to 20 minutes twice daily. While concentrating on breathing, the patient silently repeats a simple word or phrase of personal significance with each exhalation. Research suggests that, if done consistently, this practice has demonstrable physiologic as well as psychological benefits.

Exercise has been increasingly recommended as an aid to mental well-being as well as to physical health. While not a panacea, it may help persons in mild to moderate emotional distress.[11] Keep in mind, however, that exercise can *worsen* the symptoms of panic disorder.

Getting proper rest seems to be a simple goal, but it eludes many people. As an initial step, the physician can prescribe good sleep hygiene—taking time to unwind, lying down only when tired, and, with the exception of sexual activity, using the bed only to sleep and not to read, watch TV, or worry. A patient who cannot fall asleep within a short time should get up, work or read for a while, and then return to bed. The patient should go to bed at the same time every evening and get up at the same time every morning. Patients who have trouble sleeping at night should not nap during the day.[12]

Although this advice about diet, exercise, and rest seems to be common sense, patients may follow it more closely when it is presented as a physician's direction, especially if the physician is very specific in the directions. The patient's failure to implement or inability to comply with the recommendations should alert the physician to the possibility of more serious difficulties.

Progressive muscular relaxation. In progressive muscular relaxation, the patient first tenses and then releases sets of muscle groups throughout the body. With practice and repetition for 15 to 20 minutes twice daily, most patients become notably less anxious. This technique can be used alone or in combination with other techniques.[13]

Self-hypnosis. Self-hypnosis helps the patient relax deeply, combats generalized anxiety, and allows the patient to fall asleep more easily and sleep better.

Biofeedback. Biofeedback uses visual and auditory signals derived from biological measures, enabling patients to learn how to monitor and modify their biological responses.[14] Biofeedback techniques are useful for a variety of psychophysiologic disorders including generalized anxiety.

Few primary care physicians will have the time, expertise, or interest to implement these strategies themselves with anxious patients. Nevertheless, it is useful to tell patients that such approaches exist; the physician can review the options and, when appropriate, refer patients to practitioners who do use such treatment methods. The physician can also recommend appropriate self-help books and audio- or videotapes.

References

1. Schmidt DD: Patient and compliance: the effect of the doctor as a therapeutic agent. *J Fam Pract* 1977;4(5):853-856.
2. Parad HJ, Caplan G: A framework for studying families in crisis. In Parad HJ (ed): *Crisis Intervention*; selected readings. New York, Family Service Association of America, 1965.
3. Rako SM, Mazer HE (eds): *Semrad: The Heart of a Therapist*. New York, Aronson, 1980.
4. Gelder M: Behavior therapy for neurotic disorders. *Behav Modif* 1979;3:469-495.
5. Heinrich RL: Behavioral approaches to the evaluation and treatment of anxiety disorders. In Pasnau RO (ed): *Diagnosis and Treatment of Anxiety Disorders*. American Psychiatric Press, Washington, DC, 1984.
6. Marks I: *Cure and Care of the Neuroses*. New York, John Wiley and Sons, 1981.
7. Beck AT, Emery G: *Anxiety Disorders and Phobias: A Cognitive Perspective*. New York, Basic Books, 1985.
8. Christie-Seely J: Teaching the family system concept in family medicine. *J Fam Pract* 1981;13:391-401.
9. Broder E: Assessment: The foundation of family therapy. *Can Fam Physician* 1975; 21-53.
10. Carrington P: Modern forms of meditation. In Woolfolk RL, Lehrer PM (eds): *Principles and Practice of Stress Management*. New York, Guilford Press, 1984, pp 103-141.
11. Callen KE: Mental and emotional aspects of long-distance running. *Psychosomatics* 1983; 24(2):133-151.
12. Kales A, Kales JD: *Evaluation and Treatment of Insomnia*. New York, Oxford University Press, 1984.
13. Bernstein DA, Given BA: Progressive relaxation: abbreviated methods. In Woolfolk RL, Lehrer PM (eds): *Principles and Practice of Stress Management*. New York, Guilford Press, 1984, pp 43-69.
14. Budzynski TH, Stoyva JM: Biofeedback methods in the treatment of anxiety and stress. In Woolfolk RL, Lehrer PM (eds): *Principles and Practice of Stress Management*. New York, Guilford Press, 1984, p 188-219.

In recent years, research observations have provided a new understanding of the biological basis for pharmacologic treatment of anxiety. Properly prescribed medication can often control many of the symptoms of an anxiety disorder, and can facilitate the success of psychotherapy and other forms of nonpharmacologic treatment. Thus, medication should be viewed as one possible component of a comprehensive biopsychosocial approach to treatment that might include supportive counseling, patient education, lifestyle adjustments, behavioral intervention, psychotherapy, or other measures, as appropriate.

An accurate diagnosis and careful identification of therapeutic targets are essential to successful therapy. Primary care physicians see patients in all stages of evolving anxiety disorders. Even after a thorough evaluation, many patients do not meet strict diagnostic criteria for specific disorders. In such situations, treatment must be initiated on the basis of the "best-fit diagnosis." Subsequent visits should be used to observe the evolution of the disorder, reassess the target symptoms and the patient's response to treatment, and clarify diagnosis.

PATIENT SELECTION

Anxiety is a fundamental and universal human experience; anxiety *disorders* are not. Thus, a key question for the primary care physician is: "When is anxiety clinically important enough to warrant therapeutic intervention?" There is no simple formula for answering that question; but in general, treatment may be indicated when anxiety symptoms are severe, persistent, recurrent, or have a significantly disruptive effect on the patient's daily life. Specific *pharmacologic* treatment should be considered when:

- The patient's symptom cluster is consistent with a specific anxiety disorder for which medication is appropriate.

- The use of medication could prevent the development of complications (such as agoraphobia in panic disorder).

- An assessment of all the factors in the individual case (including the patient's personality, willingness to cooperate, risk of suicide, risk of drug habituation, age, coexisting medical illnesses, etc.) indicates that the potential benefits of medication outweigh the potential risks.

The patient's perception of anxiety should not be the sole foundation for pharmacologic treatment decisions. In some anxiety disorders (e.g., panic disorder), the presence and severity of symptoms may sometimes be unrelated to stressors or conflicts, and subjective awareness of anxiety may even be absent. Therefore, *characteristic symptom clusters should be the key criteria to use in initiating treatment and monitoring ongoing care.*

MEDICATION SELECTION AND DOSE TITRATION

Rational pharmacologic treatment consists of choosing both the right medication *and* the right dosage to achieve the best

---

GUIDELINES FOR RATIONAL PHARMACOLOGIC TREATMENT

- Establish an accurate diagnosis.

- Identify the target symptoms.

- Select the most appropriate agent.

- Obtain informed consent.

- Initiate therapy at a low dose.

- Increase dosage gradually, as needed.

- Aim for optimal control of symptoms with a minimal level of side effects.

- Measure progress by periodic reassessment of the target symptoms.

- After an appropriate interval, attempt to discontinue medication by tapering slowly.

- Provide continuing supportive counseling and frequent follow-up.

outcome for each patient. The clinician should begin by identifying the target symptoms and then select a therapeutic agent that effectively treats them.

Medications from a variety of classes have been used to treat the symptoms of anxiety disorders; the major ones are represented in Table 1. Some of the agents listed have not received formal FDA approval for the indications discussed here; however, published studies and clinical experience support their inclusion as possible therapeutic options.

Pharmacologic efficacy must be balanced against side effects. One of the most common reasons for noncompliance and subsequent treatment failure is the emergence of side effects deemed unacceptable by the patient. On the other hand, inadequate dosage is also a leading cause of nonresponse. The ideal dosage for a given patient can be influenced by a variety of factors, including concomitant use of other medications or alcohol, medical illnesses, previous drug sensitivities, age, and individual metabolic differences. Thus, dosage must be individualized, and careful titration is essential.

Therapy should be initiated at a low dose, with gradual increases as needed

Table 1
Dosage Ranges of Pharmacologic Agents Used in Anxiety Disorders

Agent	Usual Starting Dosage (mg)	Usual Total Daily Dosage Range* (mg)
BENZODIAZEPINES		
Alprazolam (Xanax®)	0.25–0.5 tid	0.75–4.0
Chlordiazepoxide (Librium®)	5 bid or tid	15–100
Clorazepate (Tranxene®)	7.5–15 qd	15–60
Diazepam (Valium®)	2 bid–qid	4–40
Halazepam (Paxipam®)	20 qd or bid	40–160
Lorazepam (Ativan®)	1 bid or tid	2–6
Oxazepam (Serax®)	10 tid	30–90
Prazepam (Centrax®, Verstran®)	10 qd	20–60
NONBENZODIAZEPINE ANXIOLYTIC		
Buspirone (BuSpar®)	5 tid	15–60
TRICYCLIC ANTIDEPRESSANTS†		
Desipramine (Norpramin®, Pertofrane®)	25–50	150–300
Imipramine (Tofranil®)	25–50	150–300
Trimipramine (Surmontil®)	25–50	150–300
MAO INHIBITOR†		
Phenelzine (Nardil®)	15	45–90
BETA BLOCKER		
Propranolol (Inderal®)	10	10–40

*In some anxiety disorders, higher doses may be required for some patients. Consultation with a specialist may be desirable if the physician is unfamiliar with high-dose therapy.

†Other medications in this class have also been used in the treatment of anxiety disorders; however, their effectiveness has not been proven in well-controlled studies.

and tolerated. The interval between dosage increments should equal the time it takes the medication to achieve a steady state (constant blood level); for many medications, this interval is several days. Each increment should be small, usually not exceeding 25 to 50 percent of the previous total daily dose.

During the upward titration process, tolerance to side effects usually develops. The best approach is to continue raising the dose gradually, until a balance is reached between side effects and benefits. In most cases, an optimal dosage can be found at which side effects are absent or acceptably mild and therapeutic benefits become stable, without further need for dosage increments. When long-term treatment is indicated, dosage requirements may decrease over time. Thus, long-term follow-up should include regular reevaluation of dosage as well as the need for continuing treatment.

Apparent failure to respond to treatment does not necessarily indicate a true lack of response to the selected agent (see Box). A number of issues should be reviewed, including: diagnosis, personality factors, compliance, concomitant drug use or illness, and the patient's understanding of the disorder and its treatment. In addition, therapeutic effects may be delayed. It is premature to declare a treatment failure in a chronic disorder before adequate dosage has been continued for at least four to six weeks. In a patient with a true pharmacologic nonresponse, another medication from the same or a different class may ultimately prove successful.

Patient education is a vital part of any pharmacologic treatment regimen (see the patient information aids in the Appendix). The patient who understands the nature of the disorder being treated, as well as the expected benefits and possible side effects of the prescribed medication, is more likely to comply with the physician's instructions—and, thus, more likely to have a successful outcome.

The classes of medications most commonly used in anxiety disorders are discussed below. For more detailed information on specific agents, consult the manufacturers' package inserts and the references cited in this chapter. Treatment of specific anxiety disorders is discussed more fully in Part Two of this Handbook.

BENZODIAZEPINES

During the past 20 years, benzodiazepines have replaced barbiturates and other sedative-hypnotics in the treatment of anxiety, representing a significant advance in terms of safety and decreased potential for addiction. Benzodiazepines demonstrate consistent efficacy with less sedation, fewer adverse effects and drug interactions, and a generally safer therapeutic profile than the barbiturates. As anxiolytics, benzodiazepines appear to be most effective in patients with more severe forms of anxiety. In addition, benzodiazepines have been used as sedative-hypnotics, anticonvulsants, muscle relaxants, and amnestic agents. Because of their varying pharmacokinetic properties and differences in specific effects (see Table 2),[1-6] benzodiazepines offer the clinician a range of therapeutic choices.

POSSIBLE REASONS FOR NONRESPONSE TO PHARMACOLOGIC TREATMENT

- Noncompliance
- Subtherapeutic dosage (below usual therapeutic range or below patient's requirements)
- Delayed response
- Uptake failure (e.g., malabsorption)

- Concurrent use of other drugs
- Concurrent medical illness
- Incorrect or incomplete diagnosis
- Complicating psychosocial factors
- True nonresponse

When a benzodiazepine is clinically effective, symptomatic relief often appears within a few days and becomes optimal within four to six weeks. The minimum effective dosage should be used, and regular follow-up visits should be scheduled to monitor response, compliance, and side effects, as well as to reassess the need for continued treatment. The GABA/benzodiazepine receptor complex gradually adapts to continuous benzodiazepine therapy; thus, medication should be tapered *gradually* before discontinuation (see pages 38–39).

Absorption. Although all of the benzodiazepines are well absorbed from the gastrointestinal tract, their rates of absorption differ.[1] The interval between oral administration and peak concentration can range from 30 minutes for diazepam to four hours for prazepam. Rapidly absorbed agents, such as diazepam and clorazepate, have a rapid onset of therapeutic effects. However, some patients may feel a rapid onset of subjectively undesirable drowsiness and muscle relaxation. For these patients, a more slowly absorbed benzodiazepine may be preferable.

Lipophilicity. The lipophilicity (or lipid solubility) of a benzodiazepine also influences onset of action as well as duration of effect after a single dose.[1] The more lipophilic benzodiazepines (e.g., diazepam) cross the blood-brain barrier more rapidly, but are also distributed more rapidly to peripheral tissues (primarily adipose tissue). Thus, their central effects diminish more rapidly. Effective brain concentrations of less lipophilic benzodiazepines (e.g., lorazepam) may be maintained longer after a single dose since less peripheral distribution occurs.

This explains why elimination half-life is not the only useful measure of duration of action. After a single dose, a benzodiazepine with a long elimination half-life (e.g., diazepam) may have a shorter duration of action than a benzodiazepine with a shorter elimination half-life (e.g., lorazepam), due to differences in lipophilicity and resultant distribution.[1] Thus, duration of action—as well as half-life—should be used to guide dosage schedules and evaluation of symptoms during extended maintenance therapy and upon gradual discontinuation of treatment.

Table 2
Benzodiazepine Pharmacokinetics

Agent	Lipophilicity	Absorption	Metabolic Pathway	Active Metabolites
Alprazolam (Xanax®)	Intermediate	Intermediate	Oxidation	Alpha-hydroxy-alprazolam
Chlordiazepoxide (Librium®)	Intermediate	Intermediate	Oxidation	Desmethylchlordiazepoxide, desmoxepam, desmethyldiazepam, oxazepam
Clorazepate (Tranxene®)	Intermediate to high	Rapid	Oxidation	Diazepam, desmethyldiazepam, oxazepam
Diazepam (Valium®)	High	Rapid	Oxidation	Desmethyldiazepam, oxazepam
Halazepam (Paxipam®)	Intermediate to high	Intermediate to slow	Oxidation	Desmethyldiazepam, oxazepam
Lorazepam (Ativan®)	Low	Intermediate	Conjugation	None
Oxazepam (Serax®)	Low	Intermediate to slow	Conjugation	None
Prazepam (Centrax®, Verstran®)	Intermediate to high	Slow	Oxidation	Desmethyldiazepam, oxazepam

BENZODIAZEPINE THERAPY

Advantages:

Effective

Safe

Few adverse drug interactions

Favorable sleep profile

Disadvantages:

CNS side effects may be subtle/may mimic psychiatric disease

Agents with active metabolites may accumulate in elderly or medically ill patients

Additive CNS depression when taken with alcohol

Potential for psychological/physiologic dependency

Some potential for abuse

General Prescribing Guidelines

- Use as an adjunct to lifestyle modification, relaxation therapy, psychotherapy, or other non-pharmacologic measures.

- Whenever appropriate, minimize duration of therapy or use intermittently.

- Target and monitor specific symptoms.

- Prescribe the minimum effective dose.

- Limit quantity prescribed and number of refills.

- Agents without active metabolites may be preferable in elderly or medically ill patients.

- Exercise caution in dependency-prone patients.

- Maintain frequent contact with patient.

Metabolism. Benzodiazepines are metabolized via one of two hepatic pathways—oxidation or conjugation.[1] Oxidation may produce active metabolites with a long duration of action. (For example, desmethyldiazepam is a long-acting metabolite of diazepam, chlordiazepoxide, clorazepate, halazepam, and prazepam.) Benzodiazepines with active metabolites are more sensitive to factors that may alter metabolism, such as aging, hepatic dysfunction, and concurrent drug use. In the presence of such factors, dosage adjustment is commonly required, or an agent without active metabolites may be preferred.

Benzodiazepines metabolized by conjugation (e.g., oxazepam, lorazepam), which have no active metabolites, as well as certain benzodiazepines metabolized by oxidation that have minor active metabolites (e.g., alprazolam), are less sensitive to aging, hepatic function, and concurrent drug use; however, they are more sensitive to renal insufficiency.

Common side effects. Benzodiazepines can cause dose-related side effects including sedation, behavioral disinhibition, depression, confusion, incoordination/ataxia, memory problems, and paradoxical irritability. These effects can be subtle and may be mistaken for other processes, especially in the elderly. Patients should avoid driving or engaging in other potentially hazardous activities until they have become familiar with their reactions to the medication.

Contraindications. Benzodiazepines are contraindicated in patients with acute narrow angle glaucoma or with a known hypersensitivity to any benzodiazepine. Relative contraindications include a history of alcoholism or other drug abuse.

Interactions. Benzodiazepines may produce additive CNS depressant effects if taken concurrently with alcohol, psychotropic medications, anticonvulsants, antihistamines, or other depressant drugs.

NONBENZODIAZEPINE ANXIOLYTIC

Buspirone (BuSpar®) is the first member of a new class of anxiolytics (the azaspirodecanediones) to become available in the United States. It is unrelated to the benzodiazepines, is free of muscle relaxant and sedative effects, and appears to have little or no potential for dependency. Its most common side effects are headache, light-headedness, and nausea. Buspirone has a delay of up to two weeks in onset of clinical efficacy, and it may be useful for patients with chronic anxiety disorders.[7]

TRICYCLIC ANTIDEPRESSANTS

Tricyclic antidepressants have shown promise in the treatment of certain anxiety disorders.[8-15] Imipramine (Tofranil®), the best studied tricyclic, has a robust effect on symptoms of panic attack, but is less effective for anticipatory anxiety in panic disorder with agoraphobia. Clomipramine (Anafranil®), a tricyclic antidepressant not yet available in the United States, has shown promise in obsessive-compulsive disorder.[16-20]

Tricyclic antidepressants produce varying degrees of sedative and anticholinergic effects (see Table 3).[21] They can also be divided into two categories according to their predominant effects on neurotransmitters. The older dimethylated tricyclics (e.g., amitriptyline, doxepin, imipramine) have predominant serotonin reuptake blocking properties, but also have a relatively high potential for side effects. The monomethylated tricyclics (e.g., desipramine, nortriptyline) have more prominent effects on norepinephrine and relatively less frequent side effects.

Therapy with tricyclic antidepressants should be initiated at a low dosage (e.g., 25 to 50 mg/day of imipramine or equivalent). Dosage should be increased gradually in increments of 25 to 50 mg/day every two to five days, as tolerated, while the patient is observed for signs of clinical improvement. Effective therapeutic dosages in certain anxiety disorders appear to be similar to those used in treating major depression (i.e., 150 to 300 mg/day of imipramine or equivalent). Therapeutic drug plasma monitoring may be useful in evaluating patients who fail to respond to usual dosage ranges; further upward titration may be indicated in patients with subtherapeutic levels. Up to six weeks of treatment may be required before an optimal response is achieved. Patients with anxiety disorders may experience an *increase* in anxiety during the first week or two of tricyclic therapy; however, this effect often remits thereafter and is not necessarily a reason for stopping the medication.

In responsive patients, after two or more months of clinical stability, dosage may be reduced gradually (by 25 to 50 mg every two weeks) to a maintenance level of 50 to 75 mg/day of imipramine or equivalent. If symptoms reemerge, the previous therapeutic dosage should be reinstituted for two or more months before a second attempt at dosage reduction. In patients with frequent recurrences, long-term prophylactic treatment is both safe and effective. In assessing recurrences, the physician should evaluate compliance and look for any changes in psychosocial stress factors, concomitant drug use, or physical illness.

Common side effects. The most common side effects of the tricyclic antidepressants

Table 3
Sedative and Anticholinergic Properties of Tricyclics

Agent	Sedative Effects	Anticholinergic Effects
Amitriptyline	Pronounced	Very pronounced
Desipramine	Mild	Mild to moderate
Doxepin	Pronounced	Pronounced
Imipramine	Moderate	Pronounced
Nortriptyline	Moderate	Moderate
Protriptyline	Moderate	Very pronounced
Trimipramine	Pronounced	Pronounced

TRICYCLIC ANTIDEPRESSANT THERAPY

Advantages:

Minimal abuse potential

No physiologic dependency

Disadvantages:

Anticholinergic and sedative side effects

Delayed onset of therapeutic action

Dangerous or fatal in overdose

General Prescribing Guidelines

- Initiate therapy at a low dosage (e.g., 25-50 mg/day).

- Increase dosage gradually in increments of 25-50 mg/day every two to five days.

- Schedule dosage q.h.s. when possible.

- Continue medication at least 4-6 weeks at therapeutic dosage levels before making a final assessment of efficacy.

- In responsive patients, treat for 2 or more months after full response and taper gradually (by 25-50 mg every 2 weeks).

are anticholinergic reactions (dry mouth, blurred vision, constipation, mydriasis, urinary retention) and sedation. Cardiovascular effects, including tachycardia, arrhythmias, conduction disorders, and ECG changes, have been reported with tricyclics and appear to be more common in patients with preexisting cardiac disease or toxic concentrations. Pretreatment and periodic ECG monitoring is recommended in all patients who may be at risk of cardiovascular side effects. In addition, most patients over the age of 40 should receive ECG screening before initiation of tricyclic therapy. Other common side effects reported with tricyclics include orthostatic hypotension, photosensitivity, diaphoresis, weight gain, and interference with sexual function. Patients should avoid driving or engaging in other potentially hazardous activities until they have become familiar with their reactions to the medication.

Since side effects are common during tricyclic therapy, the physician should routinely inquire about them, encourage patients to bear with them because they often subside over time, and suggest symptomatic remedies.[22]

Contraindications. Tricyclic antidepressants are contraindicated in patients with known hypersensitivity to agents of this class or during the acute recovery period following myocardial infarction. Tricyclics should be used with caution in patients with a history of cardiac disease, increased intraocular pressure, narrow angle glaucoma, urinary retention, or seizure disorders. Since the tricyclics are dangerous—sometimes fatal—in overdose, they should be prescribed with extreme caution in suicidal patients.

Interactions. Tricyclics may produce additive CNS depression in combination with alcohol or other depressants. Concurrent use of cimetidine (Tagamet®) may significantly raise tricyclic blood levels. Additive anticholinergic effects may occur with concurrent use of other anticholinergic agents. Tricyclics should not be combined with MAO inhibitors except in special circumstances, with special precautions, and under the supervision of a physician who is familiar with using the combination.

MONOAMINE OXIDASE (MAO) INHIBITORS

MAO inhibitors act by interrupting the breakdown of the centrally active mono-

MAO INHIBITOR THERAPY

Advantages:

Minimal abuse potential

No physiologic dependency

Anticholinergic side effects are less common

Disadvantages:

Necessity for dietary and drug restrictions to avoid the possibility of acute hypertensive reactions

Miscellaneous side effects

Delayed onset of therapeutic action

General Prescribing Guidelines

- Initiate therapy at a low dosage (e.g., 15 mg/day of phenelzine); titrate as needed and tolerated.
- Monitor blood pressure frequently.
- Emphasize strict observance of dietary and drug restrictions.

amines, and they may have additional mechanisms of action as yet undefined. These agents may be the drugs of first choice in the treatment of "atypical depression" (characterized by hyperphagia, hypersomnia, and *a high level of coexisting anxiety*). They have also been used to treat other types of depression, depressive equivalents such as atypical facial pain, and phobic disorders—especially panic disorder with agoraphobia.[9,23-26] Phenelzine (Nardil®) may be the most effective medication for severe, chronic cases of panic disorder refractory to treatment with benzodiazepines or tricyclic antidepressants.[27]

Initial dosage of MAO inhibitors should be low (e.g., 15 mg/day of phenelzine), with gradual increases over several weeks to minimize side effects while therapeutic response is assessed. At least three to four weeks of treatment are often required before beneficial effects appear. MAO inhibitors have fewer subjectively unpleasant side effects than the tricyclics; anticholinergic reactions are less common, and many patients experience little or no sedation. The major disadvantage of the MAO inhibitors is the necessity for strict dietary and drug restrictions. Hypertensive crises may occur if patients ingest foods or beverages high in tyramine or tryptophan or take prescription or nonprescription medications with sympathomimetic activity (see Table 4). Symptoms of hypertensive crisis may include headache, palpitations, nausea and vomiting, sweating, and tachycardia. Although many patients ingest restricted foods without untoward effects, the reactions are unpredictable and all patients should be warned about possible complications.

Common side effects. MAO inhibitors may cause orthostatic hypotension, retarded ejaculation in males, anorgasmia in females, dizziness, fatigue, paresthesias, and weight gain.

Contraindications. MAO inhibitors are contraindicated in patients with a known hypersensitivity to agents of this class, impaired liver or renal function, congestive heart failure, or pheochromocytoma. They should also be avoided in patients taking medications that could interact adversely with MAO inhibitors and in patients with a history of drug abuse.

Interactions. MAO inhibitors may interact adversely with a variety of drugs including sympathomimetics, meperidine

Table 4
Dietary and Drug Restrictions
for MAO Inhibitor Therapy

The following foods, beverages, and drugs must be avoided during MAO inhibitor therapy *and for two weeks after discontinuation:*

Meat and fish
- Meats prepared with tenderizers
- Meat extracts
- Smoked or pickled fish
- Beef or chicken liver
- Dry sausage (Genoa salami, hard salami, pepperoni, bologna)

Fruits and vegetables
- Canned figs
- Broad bean (fava bean) pods
- Bananas and avocados (especially if overripe)

Dairy products
- Cheese and foods containing cheese, such as cheese crackers and pizza (cottage cheese and cream cheese are allowed)
- Yogurt
- Sour cream

Beverages
- Beer, red wine, and other alcoholic beverages

Miscellaneous
- Soy sauce
- Yeast extract (including brewer's yeast in large quantities)
- Excessive amounts of chocolate and caffeine
- Spoiled or improperly refrigerated, handled, or stored protein-rich foods such as meats, fish, and dairy products
- Foods that have undergone protein changes by aging, pickling, fermentation, or smoking

Drugs*
- Sympathomimetics
- Meperidine
- Narcotics and other CNS depressants
- Anti-parkinsonism agents
- Antihypertensives
- Nonprescription preparations containing ephedrine or similar agents

*MAO inhibitors may interact adversely with a wide variety of drugs. Consult complete prescribing information before using any medication in combination with an MAO inhibitor.

(Demerol®), narcotics and other CNS depressants, anti-parkinsonism agents, and antihypertensives. MAO inhibitors should not be used in combination with tricyclic antidepressants except in special circumstances and with special precautions, and two different MAO inhibitors should never be given concurrently.

BETA BLOCKERS

Beta-blocking agents such as propranolol (Inderal®), 10 to 40 mg taken 45 to 60 minutes before a feared activity, have helped patients overcome "stage fright," "examination nerves," or other circumscribed social phobias.[28] Beta blockers can reduce certain autonomic responses, such as tachycardia, hyperventilation, and tremor, associated with performance anxiety, although other physical and psychological symptoms may be minimally affected.[28-30]

When used in a single dose for performance anxiety, beta blocker side effects are typically limited to fatigue. Contraindications include a history of bronchial asthma, congestive heart failure, and significant bradycardia.

SPECIAL CLINICAL SITUATIONS

Pregnancy

Benzodiazepines are capable of crossing the placenta and may accumulate in fetal tissue during continuous use of higher doses by the mother during pregnancy. An increased risk of congenital malformations and perinatal adverse effects has been reported,[31] but the association has not been proven.[32] Continuous benzodiazepine use during the third trimester of pregnancy may result in a withdrawal syndrome in the newborn. Tricyclic antidepressants have been associated with several single-case reports of various anomalies in the newborn, although subsequent studies failed to find any such association.[33] MAO inhibitor use in pregnancy has not been studied. Clearly, benzodiazepines, tricyclic antidepressants, MAO inhibitors, and other medications should be avoided during pregnancy unless they are absolutely indicated.

The Geriatric Patient

Pharmacologic therapy can be a safe, effective means of relieving the symptoms of anxiety in the elderly. However, special precautions are indicated.

First, the possibility of drug interaction should always be kept in mind. Elderly patients may be taking multiple medications for multiple ailments. Before prescribing any medication, the physician must ascertain what other drugs — prescription or nonprescription — the patient may already be using.

Second, dosage adjustments may be required. Pharmacokinetic and pharmacodynamic changes that occur with aging may predispose the elderly patient to reduced rates of drug metabolism and elimination and perhaps greater response at the target endpoints. The presence of hepatic or renal dysfunction or concurrent drug use may further inhibit metabolism. Thus, dosage in the elderly should be low, and shorter-acting agents should be preferred over longer-acting agents. For example, benzodiazepines without active metabolites are often preferable to those with active metabolites, since the latter may be associated with drug accumulation. Tricyclic dosage is often reduced by one-half to two-thirds in elderly patients; however, average or above-average doses are sometimes necessary and safe in certain elderly patients. The less sedating, less anticholinergic tricyclics should be preferred, whenever possible. The general rule for prescribing psychotropic medication to elderly patients is: "Start low, go slow."

The Surgical Patient

Chronic benzodiazepine therapy should not be stopped abruptly (see pages 38–39), and it may not always be practical to gradually taper and discontinue benzodiazepines in chronic users prior to elective surgery. However, if the anesthesiologist is aware of the medication regimen and of the potential for enhanced CNS sedation, adverse consequences can be prevented or minimized.

Tricyclic medication can usually be withheld immediately before and after a surgical procedure. The major concerns associated with concurrent administration of tricyclics and anesthesia include enhancement of adrenergic tone secondary to reuptake blockade, enhancement of anticholinergic effects (especially urinary retention and increased intraocular pressure), and additive CNS depression.

MAO inhibitors interact adversely with a great variety of drugs. For example, they may potentiate the effects of CNS depressants; they may cause hypertensive crisis in combination with sympathomimetic agents; and they may cause a variety of serious adverse effects in combination with certain analgesics — especially meperidine. Thus, MAO inhibitor therapy should be discontinued at least 14 days prior to surgery, whenever possible.

The Multiple Substance Abuser

Patients who abuse multiple substances can be very difficult and frustrating to manage. They frequently have major medical complications ranging from cirrhosis to AIDS, and they are prone to antisocial behavior and other disturbed patterns resulting from personality disorders. Most such patients abuse alcohol along with other drugs — most notably crack, cocaine, heroin, PCP, and marijuana.

Management of the multiple substance abuser should focus serially on: (1) treatment of any acute presenting medical problem, which is often overdose, respiratory disturbance, aspiration, or endocarditis; (2) withdrawal from the abused agents; (3) treatment of any chronic illnesses or complications; and (4) long-term social and psychological rehabilitation.

Substance-abusing patients tend to comply poorly with treatment regimens and often discontinue therapy prematurely. Thus, once any life-threatening or acute problem has been dealt with, the physician should focus on motivating and educating the patient. Anxiolytics are generally contraindicated in this patient population, due to the high risk of dependency and addiction, as well as drug diversion and abuse. However, short-term, cautious use of an anxiolytic may be appropriate for specific indications, especially if it could help prevent relapse to a more dangerous drug.

ABUSE, DEPENDENCY, AND MEDICATION DISCONTINUATION

Striking contrasts exist between the typical drug-abusing patient and the typical patient with an anxiety disorder. Drug abusers may abuse sedative drugs (such as alcohol, barbiturates, benzodiazepines, and even antihistamines) in an often interchangeable fashion, using whatever is most easily available. Such use is characteristically outside medical practice. Patients with anxiety disorders, on the other hand, often use benzodiazepines with restraint and dosage stability. They may take less than the maximum dose prescribed, and may reduce their dosage and dosage frequency over time.

Recent experiments offer some tentative explanations for these contrasting profiles. In double-blind studies of "drug preference," normal subjects and patients with anxiety disorders found benzodiazepines to be no more attractive than placebo; in fact, they often *preferred* the placebo. However, drug abusers rated benzodiazepines more attractive than placebo (but less attractive than shorter-acting barbiturates such as secobarbital or stimulants such as amphetamines).[34] The difference may be based on the subjects' differing reactions to the sedative effect associated with acute administration of any central nervous system depressant. Normal subjects and anxious patients may find the sedative effect undesirable. Drug abusers often like it; in fact, they seek it out.

Tolerance develops to the sedative effect produced by benzodiazepines within a few doses. In contrast, clinically significant tolerance to the anxiolytic effect does not appear even with prolonged administration of benzodiazepines.[35,36] Thus, anxious patients usually do not escalate their dosage once the final effective level has been established. Patients who abuse drugs are seeking the sedative effect; thus, as tolerance to the sedative effect develops, they escalate their dosage, use unstable dosage patterns, and often combine benzodiazepines with other sedating drugs (especially alcohol).

Abuse, psychological dependency, and physiologic adaptation to benzodiazepines are distinct phenomena, although they are often confused. Abuse is more common among patients with a history of alcoholism or other substance abuse, and it is associated with characteristic non-medical usage patterns. Psychological dependency may be more common among patients with anxiety associated with situational stressors, psychological conflicts, or dependent personality problems; these patients may substitute anxiolytic medication for conflict resolution. Physiologic adaptation (manifested by withdrawal symptoms upon medication discontinuation), in contrast, appears to occur at the level of the GABA/benzodiazepine receptor complex during long-term treatment. (See Etiology in Part One for more information on GABA.) Thus, withdrawal symptoms can occur in the absence of abuse or psychological dependency. The physician can reduce the risk of abuse or dependency through careful screening of candidates for benzodiazepine therapy. In addition, with a carefully executed discontinuation program, withdrawal symptoms can usually be minimized or prevented.

Discontinuing Benzodiazepine Therapy

Physiologic adaptation during long-term benzodiazepine use has been associated with withdrawal symptoms upon discontinuation of the medication. Several other pharmacologic agents, including beta blockers and corticosteroids, can also produce physiologic adaptation and may be associated with withdrawal symptoms if abruptly discontinued. When benzodiazepine withdrawal symptoms occur, they are usually mild and transient.[37] However, the symptoms may be more intense if any of the following factors are present:

- Dosage has been high.
- Dosage reduction is rapid.
- The patient has a high level of non-anxiety psychopathology.
- The patient receives little or no support from a physician during discontinuation.
- The benzodiazepine use has been prolonged.
- The patient has been abusing other drugs while taking benzodiazepines.

Of these six factors, the most important appear to be duration of use and concomitant abuse of other drugs. In most cases, when symptoms of benzodiazepine withdrawal occur, they peak less than two weeks after medication discontinuation and disappear within a month.[38]

Many patients on long-term benzodiazepine therapy eventually do well after gradual dosage reduction and discontinuation. Others experience a return of the original symptoms. Some of these patients might benefit from psychotherapy or other nonpharmacologic treatment. On the other hand, some long-term benzodiazepine users do well with continued treatment.[36,39] Sorting out these different groups is an important clinical challenge not easily reduced to a simple formula.

In patients with anxiety disorders, relapse is common after discontinuation of benzodiazepines, and it is sometimes difficult to distinguish symptoms of relapse from symptoms of withdrawal. The best clues involve the nature of the symptoms and the time frame of their appearance. Patients may perceive withdrawal symptoms as being different from their pretreatment symptoms of anxiety. Withdrawal symptoms are often perceptual, muscular, and gastrointestinal, and may include concentration difficulties, perceptual changes, confusion, depersonalization, tinnitus, paresthesias, involuntary motor movements, abdominal discomfort, and (infrequently) seizures. A comparison with the patient's initial target symptoms can often help clarify whether an actual relapse or a temporary withdrawal syndrome is present.

Withdrawal symptoms and symptoms of relapse have characteristic time frames. In most cases, withdrawal symptoms appear between two and 10 days after the medication is stopped or the dosage is lowered (depending on the duration of action of the specific benzodiazepine), and they usually subside within a month after the dosage reaches zero. In contrast, reemergence of the original anxiety symptoms (i.e., relapse) is often gradual and builds up for weeks or months after the medication is stopped. In addition, the symptoms of relapse are often recognized by the patient as matching those that existed before treatment. Nevertheless, not all patients react according to these guidelines. Some may experience symptoms of relapse within two weeks, for example, and some may have withdrawal symptoms that resemble the original target symptoms.[38,40]

Withdrawal symptoms can occur after use of long-acting, intermediate-acting, or short-acting benzodiazepines. However, symptoms usually appear sooner with the short-acting agents and may be more intense.[39,41] Some clinicians have suggested that long-acting benzodiazepines or other medications be used to treat the withdrawal symptoms as they emerge.[42] Although this may be desirable in some cases, it is usually preferable to simply taper the current benzodiazepine gradually. After chronic therapy, the tapering process should be carried out over a longer period of time than has been customary in primary practice—i.e., over the course of *at least six to 12 weeks*, depending on the duration of action of the specific benzodiazepine.

Patients should be given a specific, structured discontinuation program as well as the physician's continuing support. The patient's fears regarding discontinuation and possible relapse should be explored and discussed. Weekly visits are helpful during the tapering process. The possible symptoms of both relapse and withdrawal should be explained to the patient, emphasizing that symptoms of both types may be "distressing" but are not "dangerous," and that if withdrawal symptoms occur, they will diminish after about two medication-free weeks and will usually disappear within a month. Significant withdrawal symptoms may indicate the need for a more conservative tapering schedule. Particularly conservative tapering schedules should be used in patients with a history of seizure disorder, because rebound seizures can occur.[43] Anticonvulsant therapy may be indicated in such patients.

Managing Long-Term Benzodiazepine Therapy

Medical use of benzodiazepines is often short-term (less than one month) or intermittent. However, long-term daily use may be appropriate in some cases.[36] In long-term treatment, the safety, efficacy, and continuing appropriateness of the regimen should be periodically reassessed.

The Treatment Assessment Checklist[44] has been designed to aid the physician in the periodic reassessment of long-term treatment. It is a useful means of identifying full-blown or incipient problems for which gradual discontinuation of benzodiazepines may be the best solution. On the other hand, if the Checklist shows that the patient is benefiting from the benzodiazepine regimen without problems, and if the patient, family monitor, and physician agree that the use of the medication is reasonable, treatment can usually be continued safely. Any patient receiving long-term benzodiazepine treatment should be seen and reassessed at regular intervals.

Long-term use of benzodiazepines needs to be understood in the context of the emerging biological understanding of anxiety disorders. Some patients with biologically based anxiety have serious and life-long symptoms that may not be adequately controlled by nonpharmacologic measures alone. In many of these patients, symptoms return when medication is stopped, and significant levels of disability can recur. In such cases, indefinite continuation of benzodiazepine use may be justified by the severity and chronicity

TREATMENT ASSESSMENT CHECKLIST: LONG-TERM BENZODIAZEPINE USE

1. **Problem being treated.** Does the problem justify continued treatment with a benzodiazepine?

   ☐ Yes ☐ No

   Has the patient significantly benefited from benzodiazepine treatment?

   ☐ Yes ☐ No

2. **Benzodiazepine use.** Does the patient's use of the benzodiazepine remain within the prescribed limits and duration of treatment?

   ☐ Yes ☐ No

   Has the patient avoided use of other prescribed or nonprescribed agents?

   ☐ Yes ☐ No

3. **Toxic behavior.** Has the patient been free of any signs of intoxication or impairment from use of the benzodiazepine medication, either alone or in combination with other agents?

   ☐ Yes ☐ No

4. **Family monitor.*** Does the patient's family monitor confirm that there have been no problems with benzodiazepine use and that the patient has benefited from use of the medication?

   ☐ Yes ☐ No

Note: Any "No" answer is a sign of trouble and may indicate the need to discontinue benzodiazepine treatment. If all answers are "Yes," the benzodiazepine use is probably safe and appropriate.

*A responsible family member who can independently assess the patient's use — and possible abuse — of benzodiazepines or other substances affecting the central nervous system.

Adapted from DuPont.[44]

of the underlying anxiety disorder and by the positive response and lack of negative effects associated with the medication. However, careful diagnosis is essential to rule out dependent personality disorder, substance abuse, or other situations in which long-term medication may be inappropriate.

Treatment of chronic anxiety, with or without medication, should not be considered by either the physician or the patient as a once-in-a-lifetime decision. Rather, it should be part of an ongoing collaborative process embracing many possible alternatives that should be explored and periodically reassessed to find the best approach for each individual patient.

References

1. Greenblatt DJ, Shader RI, Abernethy DR: Current status of benzodiazepines. *N Engl J Med* 1983;309:354-358, 410-416.
2. Van Rooyen JM, Offermeier J: Pharmacokinetics of the benzodiazepines. *S Afr Med J* 1985;68 (suppl 8):10-13.
3. Greenblatt DJ, Divoll M, Abernethy DR, et al: Benzodiazepine pharmacokinetics: An overview, in Burrows GD, Norman TR, Davies B (eds): *Drugs in Psychiatry: Antianxiety Agents* (vol 2). New York, Elsevier, 1984.
4. Richens A, Griffiths AN: Pharmacokinetic and pharmacodynamic relationships with benzodiazepines, in Iversen SD (ed): *Psychopharmacology: Recent Advances and Future Prospects.* New York, Oxford University Press, 1985.
5. Greenblatt DJ, Shader RI, Divoll M, et al: Benzodiazepines: A summary of pharmacokinetic properties. *Br J Clin Pharmacol* 1981;11(suppl):11-16.
6. Sheehan DV: Benzodiazepines in panic disorder and agoraphobia. *J Affective Disord* 1987;13:169-181.
7. Feighner JP: Buspirone in the long-term treatment of generalized anxiety disorder. *J Clin Psychiatry* 1987;48(suppl 12):3-6.
8. Klein DF, Fink M: Psychiatric reaction patterns to imipramine. *Am J Psychiatry* 1962;119:432-438.
9. Sheehan DV, Ballenger J, Jacobson G: Treatment of endogenous anxiety with phobic, hysterical, and hypochondriacal symptoms. *Arch Gen Psychiatry* 1980;37:51-59.
10. Zitrin CM, Klein DF, Woerner MG, et al: Treatment of agoraphobia with group exposure in vivo and imipramine. *Arch Gen Psychiatry* 1980;37:63-72.
11. Zitrin CM, Klein DF, Woerner MG, et al: Treatment of phobias: Comparison of imipramine hydrochloride and placebo. *Arch Gen Psychiatry* 1983;40:125-138.
12. Liebowitz MR, Fyer AJ, Gorman JM, et al: Lactate provocation of panic attacks: I. Clinical and behavioral findings. *Arch Gen Psychiatry* 1984;13:764-770.

13. Muskin PR, Fyer AJ: Treatment of panic disorder. *J Clin Psychopharmacol* 1981; 1:81-90.

14. Gorman JM: Generalized anxiety disorders. *Mod Probl Pharmacopsychiatry* 1987;22:127-140.

15. Kahn RJ, McNair DM, Lipman RS, et al: Imipramine and chlordiazepoxide in depressive and anxiety disorders. II. Efficacy in anxious outpatients. *Arch Gen Psychiatry* 1986;43:79-85.

16. Marks IM, Stern RS, Mawson D, et al: Clomipramine and exposure for obsessive-compulsive rituals. *Br J Psychiatry* 1980;136:1-25.

17. Thoren P, Asberg M, Cronholm B, et al: Clomipramine treatment of obsessive-compulsive disorder. *Arch Gen Psychiatry* 1980;37:1281-1285.

18. Anath J, Packnold JC, Van Den Steen N, et al: Double-blind comparative study of clomipramine and amitriptyline in obsessive neurosis. *Prog Neuropsychopharmacol Biol Psychiatry* 1981;5:257-262.

19. Insel TR, Murphy DL, Cohen RM, et al: Obsessive-compulsive disorder: A double-blind trial of clomipramine and clorgyline. *Arch Gen Psychiatry* 1983; 40:605-612.

20. Marks IM, Lelliott P, Basoglu M, et al: Clomipramine, self-exposure and therapist-aided exposure for obsessive-compulsive rituals. *Br J Psychiatry* 1988;152:522-534.

21. Richardson JW, Richelson E: Antidepressants: A clinical update for medical practitioners. *Mayo Clin Proc* 1984;59: 330-337.

22. Blackwell B: Antidepressant drugs: Side effects and compliance. *J Clin Psychiatry* 1982; 43(11 Pt 2):14-21.

23. Sheehan DV, Claycomb JB: The use of MAO inhibitors in clinical practice, in Manschreck TC (ed): *Psychiatric Medicine Update. Massachusetts General Hospital Review for Physicians.* New York, Elsevier, 1980.

24. Tollefson GD: Monoamine oxidase inhibitors: A review. *J Clin Psychiatry* 1983; 44:280-289.

25. Cohen RM, Campbell IC, Dauphin M, et al: Changes in alpha and beta receptor densities in rat brain as a result of treatment with monoamine oxidase inhibiting antidepressants. *Neuropharmacology* 1982; 21:293-298.

26. Tyrer P: Towards rational therapy with monoamine oxidase inhibitors. *Br J Psychiatry* 1976;128:354-360.

27. Sheehan DV, Claycomb JB, Surman OS: The relative efficacy of phenelzine, imipramine, alprazolam, and placebo in the treatment of panic attacks and agoraphobia. Presented at meeting on Biology of Panic Disorders, Boston, November 5, 1983.

28. Gorman JM, Gorman LK: Drug treatment of social phobia. *J Affective Disord* 1987; 13:183-192.

29. Hoehn-Saric R, Merchant AF, Keyser ML, et al: Effects of clonidine on anxiety disorders. *Arch Gen Psychiatry* 1981; 38:1278-1282.

30. Noyes R, Chaudry DR, Domingo DV: Pharmacologic treatment of phobic disorders.

J Clin Psychiatry 1986;47:445-452.

31. Saxen I, Saxen L: Association between maternal intake of diazepam and oral clefts. *Lancet* 1975;2:498.

32. Rosenberg L, Mitchell A, Parsells J, et al: Lack of relation of oral cleft to diazepam during pregnancy. *N Engl J Med* 1983; 309:1282-1285.

33. Rachelefsky GS, Flynt JW, Ebbin AJ, et al: Possible teratogenicity of tricyclic antidepressants, letter. *Lancet* 1972;1:838.

34. Orzack MH, Friedman L, Dessain E, et al: Comparative study of the abuse liability of alprazolam, lorazepam, diazepam, methaqualone and placebo. *Int J Addict,* in press.

35. Rickels K, Case WG, Downing RW, et al: Long-term diazepam therapy and clinical outcome. *JAMA* 1983;250:767-771.

36. Uhlenhuth EH, DeWit H, Balter MB, et al: Risks and benefits of long-term benzodiazepine use. *J Clin Psychopharmacol* 1988;8:161-167.

37. Busto U, Sellers EM, Naranjo CA, et al: Withdrawal reaction after long-term therapeutic use of benzodiazepines. *N Engl J Med* 1986;315:854-859.

38. Pecknold JC, Swinson RP, Kuch K, et al: Alprazolam in panic disorder and agoraphobia: Results of a multicenter trial: III. Discontinuation effects. *Arch Gen Psychiatry* 1988;45:429-436.

39. Rickels K, Case WG, Schweizer A, et al: Low dose dependence in chronic benzodiazepine users: A preliminary report of 119 patients. *Pharmacol Bull* 1986;22:407-415.

40. DuPont RL, Rubin R, Swinson RP, et al: Patients' reactions to discontinuation of alprazolam for treatment of panic disorder: Clinical implications. *Arch Gen Psychiatry,* in press.

41. Salzman C, Green AI: Differential therapeutics: Psychopharmacology. In: *Psychiatric Update: American Psychiatric Association Annual Review,* vol 6, Hales RE, Frances AJ (eds). Washington, DC, American Psychiatric Press, 1987, pp 415-427.

42. Smith DE, Wesson DR: Benzodiazepine dependency syndromes. *J Psychoactive Drugs* 1983;15:85-95.

43. Noyes R, DuPont RL, Pecknold JC, et al: Alprazolam in panic disorder and agoraphobia: Results from a multicenter trial: II. Patient acceptance, side effects, and safety. *Arch Gen Psychiatry* 1988;45:423-428.

44. DuPont RL: *Benzodiazepines: The Social Issues.* Rockville, Md, Institute for Behavior and Health, 1986.

With the new approach presented in this book, primary care physicians can manage the majority of patients with anxiety disorders. Referral for consultation or treatment may be indicated, however, when:

- The patient is at risk of suicide.

- The diagnosis is uncertain.

- Pharmacologic treatment (adequate doses for adequate lengths of time) or other measures fail to produce anticipated results.

- The patient requests referral.

- The patient's illness is particularly severe or disabling, or it has atypical features.

- The anxiety is a manifestation of schizophrenia, manic-depression, or another disorder that the primary care physician does not feel comfortable treating.

- The patient needs help overcoming a phobia and would benefit from referral to a phobia clinic or a behavior therapist.

- The patient's disorder coexists with substance abuse, a personality disorder, or another complicating factor.

- The patient is overwhelmed by intrapsychic conflict or stressful situations and would benefit from formal psychotherapy.

- The patient's problems are, for any reason, beyond the scope of the primary care physician's training, interest, or time constraints.

When referral is indicated, its timing and the way it is presented to the patient can be important factors in its success. If the initial complaints were chiefly somatic, the patient should understand that the medical evaluation has been thorough. It is best to mention the possibility of an anxiety disorder early on, so the patient does not come to suspect that the diagnosis was made only by "default." The more patients understand about the nature of the disorder (or the suspected disorder), the more likely they will be to cooperate with whatever measures—including referral—are recommended. Some patients have misconceptions about what mental health professionals actually do and what sort of patients they see; correcting those impressions may also be a vital part of the referral process.

Primary care physicians should em-phasize their continuing interest and involvement so that patients do not feel abandoned or "dumped." In many cases, a referral for consultation is all that is necessary, and primary care physicians—if they are so inclined—can carry out the actual treatment plan. Consultations work best, of course, when the primary care physician knows and respects the consultant. Ultimately, a decision that the patient should remain under the care of the mental health professional is best made jointly by the three parties involved—the consultant, the primary care physician, *and* the patient.

Part Two: The Anxiety Disorders

CLINICAL PRESENTATION

A diagnosis of adjustment disorder with anxious mood should be considered in patients who have symptoms of anxiety, are experiencing a major psycho-social stressor, and do not meet the criteria for an anxiety disorder. For a patient to qualify for the diagnosis of adjustment disorder, the anxiety must begin within three months of the onset of the stressor and cause occupational and/or social impairment. Adjustment disorder is not diagnosed when symptoms persist for more than six months.

TREATMENT

Nonpharmacologic Approaches

- Counseling
- Relaxation training
- Coping strategies

Pharmacologic Approaches

- A brief course of a benzodiazepine
- A tricyclic antidepressant in patients with more chronic anxiety symptoms or contraindications to benzodiazepines

CASE HISTORY 1

Mark M., a 32-year-old married junior executive, presented to his primary care physician with a lump in his right testicle. After confirming the presence of a testicular mass, the physician scheduled consultations. Both the urologist and the oncologist recommended a biopsy and possible surgical excision. Mark was scheduled to be hospitalized and undergo surgery the following week.

During the interval prior to his operation, Mark developed significant anxiety symptoms. He feared the operation would result in a diagnosis of cancer and that his future would be clouded by pain, chemotherapy, recurrent hospitalizations, loss of sexual function, infertility, and possibly a premature death. He began experiencing difficulty sleeping, nightmares, and loss of appetite. His mind wandered at work, and his productivity became impaired. Five days before his scheduled surgery, his anxiety symptoms prompted a return visit to his primary care physician.

Mark's physician evaluated Mark's new anxiety symptoms and made a diagnosis of adjustment disorder with anxious mood; he prescribed a short-term benzodiazepine regimen and planned to see Mark for follow-up after his surgery.

A diagnosis of adjustment disorder with anxious mood should be considered in patients who have symptoms of anxiety, are experiencing a major psychosocial stressor, and do not meet the criteria for an anxiety disorder. For a patient to qualify for the diagnosis of adjustment disorder, the anxiety must begin within three months of the onset of the stressor, cause occupational and/or social impairment, and persist for less than six months. Symptoms of depression may occur conjointly with anxiety symptoms. When both are present, a diagnosis of adjustment disorder with mixed emotional features is appropriate. When symptoms of depression are more prominent, a diagnosis of adjustment disorder with depressed mood or major depression should be considered.

CLINICAL PRESENTATION

The case described in Case History 1 is typical of adjustment disorder associated with an acute, medically related psychosocial stressor; that in Case History 2 typifies adjustment disorder associated with an acute, nonmedically related psychosocial stressor. Anxiety symptoms in adjustment disorder can resemble those of generalized anxiety disorder or, less frequently, panic disorder. Sleep difficulties, apprehensive rumination, autonomic hyperactivity, and stress-induced somatic symptoms are common. With acute and time-limited stressors, a relatively brief, but often intense, anxiety syndrome can develop. With more chronic psychosocial stressors, a more chronic anxiety syndrome may evolve. A diagnosis of adjustment disorder is not made when symptoms persist for more than six months; then generalized anxiety disorder is often the appropriate diagnosis.

The presence of a stressor does not exclude the possibility of another underlying disorder. The occurrence of antecedent anxiety symptoms and episodes, phobic behavior, agoraphobia, or panic attacks points to the presence of a chronic anxiety disorder that may be aggravated by transient stress.

EPIDEMIOLOGY

Despite limited epidemiologic information about adjustment disorder in primary care, the diagnosis appears to be frequent. Adjustment disorder occurs in both adolescents and adults.[1] It is the most frequent psychiatric diagnosis made with seriously physically ill patients. Studies

CASE HISTORY 2

Sarah V., a 35-year-old schoolteacher, presented to her physician with complaints of palpitations, shortness of breath, lack of appetite, fatigue, and sleep disturbances of three months' duration. During the interview, Sarah revealed that she was recently separated and going through a divorce. Because she had two small children, she considered the pros and cons before going ahead with the plans for divorce.

She felt she couldn't live with her husband anymore and was convinced she made the right decision. But she was finding it a lot harder than she had expected. Both of the children missed their father. They were seeing him on weekends, but they were upset by the separation. Sarah was worried that the quality of her work was being affected by her anxiety and fatigue.

Sarah's physician recognized Sarah's adjustment disorder with anxiety, brought on by the stresses of divorce. She provided brief counseling sessions once a week for a month and scheduled regular follow-up visits. At her physician's suggestion, Sarah joined a support group for separated and divorced people, and she found the group helpful.

have documented that adjustment disorder is usually associated with a good prognosis; at follow-up, the majority of adults had no current mental illness.[2] A study comparing patients with adjustment disorder and controls, as well as patients with other major mental disorders, found adjustment disorder to be an intermediate syndrome distinguishable from both comparison groups.[3] This finding supports the concept that if adjustment disorder persists, it may develop into another, more durable condition, such as generalized anxiety disorder.

ETIOLOGY

Psychosocial stressors. Primary care physicians frequently care for patients who are experiencing periods of extreme stress. Hospitalization, illness, surgery, and nonoperative procedures are stressful to all patients and may produce significant anxiety-related distress and morbidity in some. Coping with pain, disability, or death commonly provokes anxiety symptoms that can result in the development of adjustment disorder. Fear of cancer—even when the possibility is remote,[4] concerns about becoming a burden to family members, or acute changes in environment, such as hospitalization in a coronary care unit following a myocardial infarction, also can produce significant situational anxiety. Stressors not related to medical problems, such as marital or job difficulties, financial problems, or other personal crises, can also contribute to the development of adjustment disorder.

The number and significance of psychosocial stressors in a patient's life are important factors in determining the degree of disability. The more stressors the patient experiences at one time, and the more disturbing the stressors are to the patient, the greater the effect on the patient's ability to adjust. The Social Readjustment Rating Scale (Table 1)[5] reflects the life activities that can be stressful.

Individual vulnerability. Limited research data are available to help predict which patients experiencing stressful situations will develop anxiety-related impairment. In studies of patients undergoing surgical procedures, predictors of postoperative mental problems were found to include past mental illness, divorced or separated marital status, and low socioeconomic status.[6] Patients with a previous history of adjustment disorder

Table 1
Social Readjustment Rating Scale

Relative Rank	Life Event
1	Death of spouse
2	Divorce
3	Marital separation
4	Jail term
5	Death of close family member
6	Personal injury or illness
7	Marriage
8	Fired at work
9	Marital reconciliation
10	Retirement
11	Change in health of family member
12	Pregnancy
13	Sex difficulties
14	Gain of new family member
15	Business readjustment
16	Change in financial state
17	Death of close friend
18	Change to different line of work
19	Change in number of arguments with spouse
20	Mortgage over $10,000
21	Foreclosure of mortgage or loan
22	Change in responsibilities at work
23	Son or daughter leaving home
24	Trouble with in-laws
25	Outstanding personal achievement
26	Wife begin or stop work
27	Begin or end school
28	Change in living conditions
29	Revision of personal habits
30	Trouble with boss
31	Change in work hours or conditions
32	Change in residence
33	Change in schools
34	Change in recreation
35	Change in church activities
36	Change in social activities
37	Mortgage or loan less than $10,000
38	Change in sleeping habits
39	Change in number of family get-togethers
40	Change in eating habits
41	Vacation
42	Christmas
43	Minor violations of the law

This rating scale, which is based on one population, shows the surprising variety of life events that can be stressful to an individual. The relative rank varies markedly among individuals and populations.

Adapted with permission from Holmes and Rahe.[5]

or complicated, prolonged psychological reactions to stressors may also be at increased risk for the disorder.

TREATMENT

Treatment of adjustment disorder with anxious mood can be approached nonpharmacologically and pharmacologically. In patients who are experiencing severe incapacitating anxiety symptoms, both may be indicated. All patients, however, will benefit from supportive counseling, performed during weekly or biweekly short visits.

Nonpharmacologic Approaches

Nonpharmacologic treatment approaches to adjustment disorder with anxious mood include individual counseling, relaxation training, and mobilization of the patient's usual stress-coping mechanisms. Individual counseling by a primary care physician, trained counselor, or nurse can provide opportunities for expression of fears in a supportive environment. In some cases, laypersons who have passed through a similar illness or crisis can help decrease a patient's anxiety. Relaxation techniques may be effective in reducing some target symptoms.

It is important that the primary care physician understand the coping mechanisms normally employed by the individual who is experiencing a medically related stressor. Relief and diversion from the anxiety-provoking stimulus can be provided by enlisting the aid of a family member, the patient's minister, or a trusted friend, as well as by allowing personal possessions to be available during hospitalization. Also, by encouraging exercise and a rapid return to work, the physician can decrease the fear of disability and reinforce the expectation that recovery will occur.

Pharmacologic Approaches

Pharmacologic treatment approaches to adjustment disorder are similar to those used in managing acute symptoms in generalized anxiety disorder. Short-term treatment with a benzodiazepine can reduce anxiety and improve sleep. The doses should be adjusted to prevent oversedation. Treatment for one to three weeks often suffices. The patient should clearly understand that the medication is to be used on a regular basis and for a limited time. Tricyclic antidepressants given at bedtime can be used to promote sleep and alleviate more chronic anxiety symptoms related to psychosocial stressors, as well as to treat patients with contraindications to benzodiazepines.

MANAGEMENT

Prevention is important in the management of adjustment disorder. Many opportunities for prevention may arise, because primary care physicians frequently deal with patients who are experiencing medically and nonmedically related stressors. Prior to hospitalization or a procedure, the patient's concerns can be determined by asking open-ended questions, such as "What worries you about going into the hospital?" or "What are your fears about having an operation?" These questions allow for identification of the patient's fears. By addressing these concerns, the physician may prevent significant anxiety symptoms from developing.

Follow-up and continuity of care are especially important in the management of adjustment disorder. Because reactions to stressors can vary over several days, weekly follow-up on an outpatient basis may be necessary. Hospitalized patients with adjustment disorder can be evaluated on a day-to-day basis.

REFERRAL

Many patients with adjustment disorder can be managed successfully by primary care physicians and do not require psychiatric evaluation or psychiatric hospitalization. On the other hand, some patients with adjustment disorder (especially those with significant depressive syndromes) may be at risk for suicidal behavior. Patients who have suicidal thoughts may require psychiatric evaluation.

References

1. Andreasen NC, Wasek P: Adjustment disorders in adolescents and adults. *Arch Gen Psychiatry* 1980;37:1166-1170.
2. Andreasen NC, Hoenck PR: The predictive value of adjustment disorder in adolescents and adults. *Am J Psychiatry* 1982;139:584-590.
3. Fabrega H, Mezzich JE, Mezzich AC: Adjustment disorder as a marginal or transitional illness category in DSM-III. *Arch Gen Psychiatry* 1987;44:567-572.
4. Steptoe A, Hortt J, Stanton S: Concern about cancer in women undergoing elective gynecological surgery. *Soc Sci Med* 1986;23:1139-1145.
5. Holmes TH, Rahe RH: The Social Readjustment Rating Scale. *J Psychosom Res* 1967;11:213-218.
6. Dean C: Psychiatric morbidity following mastectomy: Preoperative predictors and types of illness. *J Psychosom Res* 1987;31:389-392.

PSYCHOSOCIAL STRESSORS

Medically Related

- Acute or chronic medical illness
- Surgical and nonsurgical procedures
- Diagnostic evaluations
- Hospitalization
- Illness of a family member
- New diagnoses
- Relapses

Nonmedically Related

- Interpersonal crises
- Marital discord, separation, divorce
- Job difficulties
- Relocation
- Financial problems
- Academic problems
- Legal problems

Symptoms of anxiety and depression frequently coexist, presenting considerable potential for diagnostic confusion. In primary care practices, especially, such symptoms may be nonspecific and diffuse, and may fail to meet strict diagnostic criteria for any single disorder. Moreover, a number of symptoms — including sleep and appetite disturbances, difficulty concentrating, irritability, and fatigue — are characteristic of both anxiety and depression. Nevertheless, when symptoms appear to be "mixed," every effort should be made to establish a primary diagnosis. Treatment should be targeted to the most prominent symptoms, and response to treatment may further clarify the diagnosis and suggest refinements in the treatment approach. Ultimately, diagnostic precision is the best foundation for effective treatment and long-term management. For more information, see Anxiety and Depression in Part One.

KEY POINTS

- Symptoms of anxiety are common in patients with major depression, and depressive symptoms are common in patients with anxiety disorders.
- When a patient presents with symptoms of both anxiety and depression, every effort should be made to establish the primary diagnosis.
- Because of the significant potential for overlap with other disorders, generalized anxiety disorder or panic disorder should not be diagnosed during a depressive episode.
- Clues to distinguishing an anxiety disorder from primary depression may include predominant mood, age of onset, sleep patterns, psychomotor signs, family history, substance use, response to exercise, and psychosocial effects.
- Secondary depression may result from progressive disability associated with a primary anxiety disorder.
- For the anxious or depressed patient, treatment should be initiated on the basis of a "best-fit" diagnosis, targeted to the most prominent symptoms.
- Response to treatment may suggest revisions in the "working" diagnosis.
- When the primary diagnosis is unclear, a tricyclic antidepressant is often the drug of first choice.
- Ultimately, diagnostic precision is the best foundation for effective treatment and long-term management of anxiety and depressive disorders.

CLINICAL PRESENTATION

Generalized anxiety disorder (GAD) is characterized by excessive cognitive anxiety associated with physical symptoms of anxiety. The prevalence of the disorder is unclear. GAD is continuous rather than episodic. Panic attacks are absent. The dominant feature of GAD is a persistent worried mood that is unrelated to another mental disorder. The worried mood persists for at least six months. Patients with GAD exhibit six or more symptoms of motor tension, autonomic hyperactivity, or vigilance and scanning (see below) and have no other disease causing these symptoms. Typical symptoms include:

- Irritability
- Difficulty falling asleep
- Diminished ability to concentrate
- Shortness of breath, palpitations, or dizziness
- Excessive sweating, flushing, or dry mouth
- Frequent urination, nausea, or diarrhea
- Muscle aches or tension
- Restlessness or trembling
- Fatigue or difficulty relaxing

Before a diagnosis of GAD can be made, panic disorder, depression, and adjustment disorder must be ruled out.

TREATMENT

Nonpharmacologic Approaches

- Supportive counseling or psychotherapy
- Self-regulatory therapies (progressive relaxation, biofeedback, or meditation)
- Behavior therapy
- Exercise

Pharmacologic Approaches

- A benzodiazepine
- A tricyclic antidepressant
- A nonbenzodiazepine anxiolytic

CASE HISTORY

Tim K., a 29-year-old graduate student, presented to his primary care physician with a mild, recurrent acneiform rash on his face and upper extremities. For the past two years, Tim had been very concerned and worried about the condition, even though he was reassured by a number of dermatologists and primary care physicians that the rash was not serious or life-threatening. No specific diagnosis, however, was made. Tim was also very worried about the quality of his current research at the university, even though he had received consistently positive evaluations by the faculty.

The rash appeared to be worse during times of stress, and Tim attributed his gradual social withdrawal and preoccupation with his appearance to the disorder. The only time the rash abated during the past two years was when Tim was on vacation, backpacking with a friend.

Tim also complained of increasing muscle tension, sweating, light-headedness, diarrhea, difficulty concentrating, easy irritability, and trouble falling asleep over the past two years.

Tim described a chaotic childhood; his parents quarreled constantly and eventually divorced. He "escaped" into scholastics, achieving a good deal of academic success. He was married for a year in his early 20s. His wife eventually divorced him and married his best friend.

Tim's primary care physician reviewed the dermatological reports, and after completing a routine physical and laboratory examination, which revealed no serious physical disease, made a diagnosis of generalized anxiety disorder. A treatment plan was discussed, and both the patient and the physician agreed to the following:

- Regular follow-up visits, weekly for the first month, less often as indicated thereafter.

- Trial of low-dose benzodiazepine therapy, with possible increase in dosage over time.

Tim responded well to the treatment, and as the anxiety symptoms diminished over the following month, his preoccupation with the rash (and the rash itself) diminished as well. Subsequently, Tim's medication was tapered gradually and discontinued.

Although generalized anxiety disorder (GAD) was formerly considered to be a common disorder, its prevalence is now unclear. Many patients who had been diagnosed with GAD were found to have panic disorder, an affective disorder such as depression or dysthymia, or adjustment disorder with anxious mood, upon careful reevaluation. Because a diagnosis of GAD cannot be made in the presence of another anxiety disorder or an affective disorder, it is very important to take a careful history to avoid making an erroneous diagnosis.

CLINICAL PRESENTATION

GAD is characterized by excessive cognitive anxiety. The disorder is continuous rather than episodic. Episodes or attacks of anxiety are absent. The dominant feature of GAD is a persistent worried mood that is unrelated to another mental disorder. The worried mood persists for at least six months. Patients with GAD worry about unfortunate events, such as accidents or illnesses, that are unlikely to occur, or have exaggerated fears about finances, their job, or their marriage. Many individuals are "keyed up" and irritable, and have difficulty falling asleep. Some find that their ability to concentrate is poor.

In addition, patients with GAD experience a variety of physical symptoms. Many are bothered by shortness of breath, palpitations, or dizziness. Others notice excessive sweating, flushing, dry mouth, frequent urination, nausea, or diarrhea. Some individuals experience tension or aching in their muscles, as well as restlessness and trembling. They may tire easily, yet have difficulty relaxing.

Anxiety symptoms commonly occur in association with other mental and physical illnesses. However, the diagnosis of GAD is made only in the absence of other anxiety disorders or physical conditions that cause anxiety, such as hyperthyroidism. Patients with generalized anxiety often have depressive symptoms as well. When these symptoms are prominent, a depressive disorder should take precedence as a diagnosis. If the patient has a history of unexpected anxiety attacks, a diagnosis of panic disorder should be made.

Although patients with GAD may complain of nervousness, they more often present with somatic complaints.[1] These may take the form of headaches or ab-

Table 1
Diagnostic Criteria for Generalized
Anxiety Disorder

A. Unrealistic or excessive worry (apprehensive expectation) about two or more life circumstances for a period of six months or longer
B. If another disorder is present, the focus of the worry is unrelated to it
C. The disturbance does not occur only during a mood disorder or a psychotic disorder
D. The presence of at least six of the following 18 symptoms:

Motor tension
(1) trembling, twitching, or feeling shaky
(2) muscle tension, aches, or soreness
(3) restlessness
(4) easy fatigability

Autonomic hyperactivity
(5) shortness of breath
(6) palpitations
(7) sweating, or cold, clammy hands
(8) dry mouth
(9) dizziness or light-headedness
(10) nausea, diarrhea, or other abdominal distress
(11) flushes or chills
(12) frequent urination
(13) trouble swallowing or "lump in throat"

Vigilance and scanning
(14) feeling keyed up or on edge
(15) exaggerated startle response
(16) difficulty concentrating
(17) trouble falling or staying asleep
(18) irritability or impatience

E. An organic factor (e.g., hyperthyroidism, caffeine intoxication) did not initiate and maintain the disturbance.

Adapted with permission from *DSM-III-R*.[2]

dominal distress. Drug or alcohol abuse may be present, especially in men. Patients with long-standing anxiety may seek treatment when symptoms intensify as a result of psychosocial stressors. Table 1 lists the diagnostic criteria for GAD.[2]

EPIDEMIOLOGY

The prevalence of GAD is unclear. As defined by the more restrictive *DSM-III-R* criteria, the disorder may be rather rare. The onset of the disorder is gradual,[3] usually beginning in the 20s, 30s, or the late teens. It tends to be chronic with a fluctuating course,[4] and is not characterized by acute, unprovoked attacks of anxiety.

ETIOLOGY

Although little is known about the cause of GAD, personality susceptibility and stressful life events appear to be important factors. Stressful life events are associated with the onset of the disorder in 50 percent of patients and may play a role in the persistence of symptoms. Events that represent a future danger are more likely to produce anxiety.[5]

TREATMENT

GAD can be a disease of long duration.[6] The goal of treatment is to reduce symptoms to a manageable level; total elimination of symptoms may not be possible. When patients exhibit mild symptoms in association with psychosocial stressors, nonpharmacologic treatment may be satisfactory and should be tried first. If more severe or persistent symptoms are present, some combination of pharmacologic and nonpharmacologic therapies may be required. Psychological treatment includes supportive psychotherapy, as well as self-regulatory and behavioral therapies. Pharmacologic treatment consists of a benzodiazepine, a tricyclic antidepressant, or a nonbenzodiazepine anxiolytic.

Treatment of patients with GAD should begin with a physical examination and reassurance regarding the absence of physical disease. These measures not only rule out more serious illness, but also relieve anxiety and help establish rapport between physician and patient. The next step is to communicate a specific diagnosis. References to "stress" or "nerves" are unsatisfactory. They convey little useful information and suggest to patients that they themselves are responsible for their condition. Symptoms should be explained clearly and simply without the use of medical jargon, and a favorable prognosis should be offered.

Nonpharmacologic Approaches

Patients seeking help for GAD often feel overwhelmed and demoralized.[7] Supportive counseling or psychotherapy can reverse these trends. Physicians may offer anxious patients an opportunity to express concerns about work or family problems, then explore possible connections between these problems and recent symptoms. Next, ways of modifying these circumstances so as to reduce symptoms may be considered. A few short sessions on a weekly basis may provide considerable relief.[8]

Other therapeutic options include self-regulatory treatments, such as relaxation, biofeedback, and meditation.[9] These strategies produce a relaxation response that can lessen anxiety and reduce the feeling of loss of control that many patients experience.[10] Their effectiveness, however, has not been proven. The method of progressive relaxation involves systematic tensing and relaxing of muscle groups. Instructions for teaching the techniques are straightforward and widely available.[11,12] Electromyographic feedback and transcendental meditation may also be useful in relieving anxiety, provided these methods are available and appeal to the patient. Like relaxation, however, these strategies take effect gradually and must be practiced regularly.

Relaxation is often combined with one or more behavior therapies to achieve greater benefit.[13] These therapies aim at modifying the avoidant behavior or anxious cognitions that accompany generalized anxiety. One behavioral strategy, known as anxiety symptom management, has several components designed to reduce anxious thoughts. These components include an explanation of anxiety symptoms, training in distraction, and practice in counterbalancing anxious thoughts with reassuring, rational ones. Descriptions of these techniques are available, and the procedures are simple to implement.[14,15]

Exercise may be beneficial to many patients with GAD. Its value should not be overlooked when formulating an overall treatment plan.

Pharmacologic Approaches

Pharmacologic treatment is indicated for patients with GAD who have more severe or persistent symptoms. Short-term therapeutic trials of up to six months should be instituted in combination with the nonpharmacologic interventions described above, with periodic attempts to taper and discontinue the medication. This approach is consistent with the natural, fluctuating course of GAD.

The benzodiazepines continue to be the most widely prescribed drugs for GAD. For example, diazepam (Valium®), 10 mg taken at bedtime, is often effective in promoting sleep and reducing daytime anxiety. However, dose adjustment, within the range of 4 to 40 mg/day, is important to maximize the benefit and minimize side effects. If necessary, one-third of the daily dose may be taken at noon. Alprazolam (Xanax®) is a higher-potency benzodiazepine that may be less sedating in equipotent dosages. The usual dosage range for alprazolam in GAD is 0.75 to 4.0 mg/day, given in divided doses. With any benzodiazepine, sedation is usually dose-related and tends to subside with a reduction in dose or continued use.

Buspirone (BuSpar®) is a nonbenzodiazepine anxiolytic that causes little sedation and appears to have little abuse potential but takes up to two weeks for the onset of anxiolytic effect.[18]

Tricyclic antidepressants are also used to treat patients with GAD, especially those who are likely to require long-term pharmacologic therapy. A sedating tricyclic given at bedtime may be effective at low dosage.[16] Tolerance to the sedative effects will occur over time. Patients must be made aware that the medication may be very sedating initially. A less sedating tricyclic may be effective at the usual antidepressant dosage (150 to 300 mg/day).[17] Because anxious patients are especially sensitive to the anticholinergic side effects of tricyclics, a dose of 25 to 50 mg/day should be given initially, then increased in 25-mg increments. The therapeutic response to this type of medication is usually delayed and occurs after the fourth week on more than 150 mg/day.

MANAGEMENT

A benzodiazepine should be taken on a regular basis for a few days to a few weeks to provide a respite from severe anxiety. During this period, factors contributing to anxiety symptoms may subside, or action may be taken to modify them. Patients may then be encouraged to reduce the dose, take the medication eventually on an as-needed basis, and ultimately discontinue their use of medication. Long-acting agents such as diazepam and prazepam (Centrax®) may be given once daily at bedtime and offer the advantage of a built-in tapering effect when stopped.[19] Even after stopping the medication, many patients are comforted by the knowledge that relief is available should they need it.

Benzodiazepines should always be discontinued gradually. The daily dose of alprazolam, for example, should be reduced by 0.25 to 0.5 mg/week or, in some patients, even more slowly — by 0.25 mg every two weeks. Patients who have taken benzodiazepines for a year or more may need support and guidance in stopping the medication. They should not interpret a reemergence of symptoms as recurrence of illness; such symptoms may subside in a week or two. Once a schedule for tapering the medication has been agreed upon, weekly visits may be desirable. If chronic anxiety symptoms reappear, alternative forms of treatment or psychiatric referral may be considered. The physician should also be alert to the substitution of alcohol for the benzodiazepine and the potential for alcohol abuse and depression, which are the most frequent complications of GAD.

PATIENT EDUCATION

Patients with GAD will benefit from an explanation of their symptoms and the factors that affect them.[20] Symptoms that are described as part of the "fight or flight" response or as the result of a surge of adrenaline may seem less alarming. Patients should also be aware that muscle tension may lead to aching, hyperventilation may lead to light-headedness and paresthesias, and symptoms may worsen in response to caffeine, nicotine, alcohol, fatigue, loss of sleep, and sometimes exercise (many patients with GAD do benefit from exercise). In addition, environmental stress usually aggravates symptoms, even though it is not the sole cause of them.

Through education, patients should be encouraged to lead active and productive lives. Some people avoid social or work activities because they contribute to anxiety. Such individuals should be urged to resist those tendencies and gradually challenge themselves in anxiety-provoking situations.

REFERRAL

Referral to a psychiatrist should be considered for patients with GAD who do not respond to pharmacologic and nonpharmacologic therapies prescribed by the primary care physician. These individuals often have significant personality or adjustment problems.[21] In addition to anxiety, such patients may experience problems with family relationships and job performance. Most individuals who need maintenance medication will not require psychiatric referral as long as the dose remains in the therapeutic range and both physician and patient agree on how the medication is to be taken. On the other hand, patients who need high doses, who have trouble discontinuing a benzodiazepine, or who abuse alcohol may benefit from referral to a psychiatrist or a substance abuse treatment facility.

References

1. Goldberg D: Detection and assessment of emotional disorders in a primary care setting. *Int J Ment Health* 1979;8:30-48.
2. American Psychiatric Association: *Diagnostic and Statistical Manual of Mental Disorders,* Third Edition — Revised. Washington, DC, American Psychiatric Association, 1987.
3. Hoeh-Saric R, McLeod DR: Generalized anxiety disorder. *Psychiatr Clin North Am* 1985;8:73-88.
4. Appenheimer T, Noyes R: Generalized anxiety disorder. *Primary Care* 1987;14:635-648.
5. Finlay-Jones R, Brown GW: Types of stressful life events and the onset of anxiety and depressive disorders. *Psychol Med* 1981;11:803-815.
6. Noyes R Jr: Natural history of anxiety disorders, in Roth M, et al (eds): *Handbook of Anxiety* (vol I). Amsterdam, Elsevier, in press.
7. Frank JD: The psychotherapy of anxiety, in Grinspoon L (ed): *Psychiatry Update* (vol 3). Washington, DC, American Psychiatric Press, 1984, pp 418-425.
8. Catalan J, Gath D, Edmonds G, et al: The effects of non-prescribing of anxiolytics in general practice. I. Controlled evaluation of psychiatric and social outcome. *Br J Psychiatry* 1984;144:593-602.
9. Goldberg RJ: Anxiety reduction by self-regulation: Theory, practice and evaluation. *Ann Intern Med* 1982;96:483-487.
10. Benson H: *The Relaxation Response.* New York, Morrow, 1975.
11. Bernstein DA, Borkovec TD: *Progressive Relaxation Training: A Manual for the Helping Professions.* Champaign, Ill, Research Press Co, 1973.
12. Davis M, et al: *The Relaxation and Stress Reduction Workbook.* San Francisco, New Harbinger Publications, 1980.

13. Deffenbacher JL, Suinn RM: Generalized anxiety syndrome, in Michelson L, Ascher LM (eds): *Anxiety and Stress Disorders, Cognitive-Behavioral Assessment and Treatment.* New York, Guilford Press, 1987, pp 352-360.
14. Suinn RM: *Manual, Anxiety Management Training.* Fort Collins, Colo, Suinn, 1977.
15. Stern RS: *Behavioral Techniques.* London, Academic Press, 1978.
16. Gorman JM: Generalized anxiety disorders. *Mod Probl Pharmacopsychiatry* 1987;22:127-140.
17. Kahn RJ, McNair DM, Lipman RS, et al: Imipramine and chlordiazepoxide in depressive and anxiety disorders. II. Efficacy in anxious outpatients. *Arch Gen Psychiatry* 1986;43:79-85.
18. Feighner JP: Buspirone in the long-term treatment of generalized anxiety disorder. *J Clin Psychiatry* 1987;48(suppl 12): 3-6.
19. Hollister LE: Prudent use of antianxiety drugs in medical practice, in *Clinical Anxiety/Tension in Primary Care Medicine.* Amsterdam, Excerpta Medica, 1979, pp 51-65.
20. Noyes R Jr: Is panic disorder a disease for the medical model? *Psychosomatics* 1987;28:582-586.
21. Rickels K: Assessment of anxiety/tension and selection for psychiatric referral, in *Clinical Anxiety/Tension in Primary Care Medicine.* Amsterdam, Excerpta Medica, 1979, pp 68-75.

CLINICAL PRESENTATION

The essential feature of obsessive-compulsive disorder (OCD) is the presence of recurrent obsessions or compulsions that are sufficiently severe to cause marked distress, consume more than an hour a day, or interfere significantly with the patient's normal routine, functioning, or relationships. Patients with OCD are identified relatively infrequently in primary care practice.

Obsessions are recurrent, intrusive, and unwanted ideas, thoughts, images, or impulses; they are described as senseless, undesirable, repugnant, or even abhorrent. Common obsessions include repetitive thoughts of violence, contamination, and doubt. Obsessions typically evoke anxiety, which leads to compulsive rituals.

Compulsions are behaviors that may seem purposeful but are performed in a ritualistic manner. The rituals are observable or mental behaviors that are repeated in a stereotypic or rule-guided manner to reduce or neutralize anxiety associated with obsessions. Common compulsions are hand-washing, checking, counting, hoarding, and touching.

TREATMENT

Nonpharmacologic Approaches

- Behavior therapy (exposure and response prevention)
- Psychotherapy

Pharmacologic Approaches

- MAO inhibitors and tricyclic antidepressants are occasionally helpful, particularly when depression is prominent.
- Neuroleptic agents are rarely effective and should be avoided.
- Benzodiazepines may be helpful only briefly during periods of intense anxiety.
- Some investigational antidepressant medications have been shown to have significant beneficial effects.

CASE HISTORY

Henry C., a 35-year-old married accountant, presented to his primary care physician with complaints related to persistent, unreasoning fear of developing AIDS (Henry had not engaged in any high-risk practices). On exploring the patient's complaints, the physician found that Henry washed his hands many times a day, and took a shower and changed his clothes up to three times a day in an effort to "stay clean and avoid contamination."

The physician diagnosed obsessive-compulsive disorder and referred Henry to a psychiatrist. The psychiatrist treated Henry with behavioral techniques (exposure and response prevention), supportive psychotherapy, and imipramine (final dose 200 mg/day). He involved Henry's wife in the treatment, and suggested the couple attend a support group for OCD patients and their families. The medication was not effective in relieving Henry's obsessions and compulsions, and was discontinued; the psychiatrist recommended trying clomipramine when it becomes available.

Henry's cleaning rituals subsided and his fear of AIDS eased somewhat but did persist. His primary care physician saw him on a monthly basis to review his symptoms, discuss his concerns, and review his physical status.

Traits such as punctuality, diligence, cleanliness, and careful organization are found and valued in many normal individuals. Such traits never become excessive in the great majority of people, but in some they may increase to the point of causing substantial dysfunction and distress. When these characteristics are present to the degree that normal functioning is impaired, the individual is said to suffer from obsessive-compulsive disorder (OCD). The disorder is identified relatively infrequently in primary care, possibly because some patients may be reluctant to reveal their repetitive obsessions and rituals.

CLINICAL PRESENTATION

OCD is characterized by obsessions or compulsions. Obsessions are intrusive and unwanted ideas, thoughts, images, or impulses that occur repeatedly. Individuals who have obsessions describe them as senseless, undesirable, repugnant, or even abhorrent, as well as intrusive and involuntary. Common obsessional themes focus on aggression (harming others, acting on an illegal impulse, causing a calamity, etc.); contamination with germs or dirt (often with bodily wastes or secretions), environmental contaminants (asbestos, toxic wastes, radiation, etc.), or household cleansers or solvents, leading to irrational fears of illness in self or others; sex (perverse sexual thoughts or impulses); loss of important possessions; religion ("blasphemous" thoughts); orderliness and symmetry; and doubt (unsure whether one has done something). Obsessions typically evoke anxiety, which, in turn, brings on compulsive rituals (see Table 1).

Compulsions are behaviors that may seem purposeful but are performed in a ritualistic manner. These rituals are observable or mental behaviors repeated in a stereotypic or rule-guided manner to reduce or neutralize anxiety associated with obsessions. Common compulsions include cleaning and washing, checking, counting, repeating, ordering/arranging, hoarding, touching, avoiding settings and other stimuli that provoke obsessions and rituals, and, quite frequently, repeatedly requesting reassurance that the thing obsessively feared has not occurred. Ninety percent of patients with the disorder exhibit both obsessions and rituals, whereas 10 percent describe only obsessive ruminations (without manifest or covert rituals).[1] Both obsessions and compulsions consume time (more than an hour a day), interfere with functioning, cause distress, and are resisted, yet are difficult for the individual to control. These five dimensions (time, interference, distress, resistance, and control) are used to diagnose OCD and to monitor change in response to treatment.

In contrast to patients with hypochondriasis or somatization disorder, insight is preserved in patients with OCD. Most patients (with the occasional exception of small children) recognize that their obsessions and ritualistic behaviors are excessive but feel powerless to respond rationally. They often fear that they will be judged "goofy, stupid, silly, irrational, insane, dumb, crazy, or bizarre" by others.

At its worst, OCD can occupy virtually every waking moment of the person's life. Furthermore, the disorder may spread to involve family members as the patient insists they comply with avoidance and rituals (such as not bringing "contaminated" friends into the home; changing "outside" for "inside" clothes; and dipping their hands in a disinfecting solution after urinating or defecating and before eating).

Specifically excluded from a diagnosis of OCD are the preoccupations with food seen in patients with eating disorders, compulsive activities that produce pleasure (such as drug use, gambling, or sexual behaviors), and depressive and schizophrenic ruminations.

A few questions directed at the issues of obsessive thinking and compulsive rituals will usually identify the presence of OCD and permit patients to describe their problem in detail. Useful questions include the following:

- Do you experience distress because of obsessive thoughts or compulsions?

- How much time do you spend with obsessions and rituals in a given day?

- How much do your obsessions and rituals interfere with your functioning in important roles?

Unless confronted with appropriate stimuli, individuals with OCD may appear less anxious than do patients with other anxiety disorders. When exposed to such stimuli, however, patients with OCD may experience intense anxiety that is obvious to all those around them.

EPIDEMIOLOGY

The Epidemiologic Catchment Area survey found that 1.5 percent of the American population (more than three million individuals) met the criteria for OCD within a six-month period[2] and 2.5 to 3 percent* had diagnosable OCD during their lifetimes.[3] OCD is equally common in men and women. Although many patients remain untreated, growing awareness of effective therapies is prompting more individuals to seek help.

In one-third of cases, OCD begins by age 15. It is not uncommon to see individuals who have struggled with the disorder for decades. The course of OCD is usually chronic, with symptoms waxing and waning.

ETIOLOGY

Understanding of the etiology of OCD is still incomplete, although various theories have proposed genetic, developmental, behavioral, psychological, and biochemical correlates for the disorder.

All thought and emotion, including obsessions and anxiety, are mediated by biochemical reactions in the brain. There is growing evidence that abnormalities of serotonin neurotransmission play a part in the pathophysiology of OCD. Recent data gathered via positron emission tomography studies suggest that patients with OCD may have increased metabolism in the orbital gyri of the frontal lobes.[4] These areas are richly supplied with serotonin neurons and support the functions of time-consciousness and social propriety. Obsessive-compulsive individuals display these characteristics to excessive degrees, whereas individuals who suffer severe frontal lobe damage (which interferes with functioning) may become disinhibited, forgetful, slothful, and socially unconcerned—traits opposite those exhibited by people with OCD.

TREATMENT

When considering management strategies for patients with OCD, the physician should remain open to all the available options. The ultimate goal of treatment is the reduction of symptoms. A combination of pharmacologic and behavioral modalities is often found to be more effective than either approach alone.

The physician might want to consider sharing the care of OCD patients with a

---

*These are reconstructed percentages from the raw data.

psychiatrist, where appropriate. In some cases, early referral to a psychiatrist or a behavior therapist skilled in exposure and response prevention or to an anxiety disorders center may be indicated.

Nonpharmacologic Approaches

The recommended nonpharmacologic approach is behavior therapy. Behavior therapy for OCD relies on common-sense techniques that can usually be taught by the primary care physician during an office visit. One study found that a total of three hours and 15 minutes of the clinician's time, spread over 17 weeks, resulted in a substantial reduction of patients' symptoms.[5]

The basic approach is to ask patients to expose themselves to the things they fear, to remain in contact with these objects or situations until their anxiety subsides, and to refrain from doing (or at least to delay) their rituals. Such ritual reduction is called "response prevention." Patients soon learn that avoidance and rituals are more time-consuming and less effective in reducing distress and dysfunction than are exposure and response prevention.

The physician should explain the principles of exposure and response prevention to help the patient prepare a hierarchy of graded exposure tasks (from easy to difficult) and design a written monitoring system, often in the form of a daily diary. The patient takes the written exposure prescription home and records the results of exposure sessions and response prevention of rituals; the duration of exposure sessions, delay in rituals, and distress experienced are documented. These diaries can be quickly and easily reviewed during the next office visit, at which time a new exposure prescription is prepared. Self-help instruction sheets, as well as self-help manuals,[6-8] may also prove useful.

Many patients may have "forgotten" how to do things normally after many years of ritualistic behavior. It may be important to have someone model normal behaviors such as showering, hand-washing, toothbrushing, food preparation, housecleaning, shopping, and so on. In addition, a family member or friend may serve as a "cotherapist," providing encouragement, helping to initiate exposure sessions and delay rituals, and praising the patient when goals are achieved.

Unlike medication, behavior therapy allows patients to apply treatment specifically to situations in which obsessions and rituals are problematic. Often, the use of self-help manuals is the only therapy required. Improvement is evident in approximately 70 percent of patients treated with exposure and response prevention. The overall reduction in compulsive symptoms is more than 50 percent.[5,9] Furthermore, greater improvement is often seen over time, as behavioral principles become habitual and are rapidly applied to any new obsessions and compulsions.

Pharmacologic Approaches

Virtually every psychoactive medication has been evaluated in the treatment of severe, persistent OCD. Monoamine oxidase inhibitors, as well as tricyclic antidepressants, are occasionally helpful, particularly when depression is prominent.

Table 1
Common Obsessions and Corresponding Compulsions

Obsessions/Fears	Compulsions/Rituals (if any)
Disease	Care seeking/checking
Contamination	Washing/cleaning
Doubt	Checking/repeating
Harming others	Checking/repeating
Losing things	Hoarding
Asymmetry/disorder	Ordering
Sexual preoccupation	——
Blasphemous thoughts	Reading the Bible

Avoidance and seeking reassurance are common rituals. For example, patients who are obsessed with a fear of germs may try to avoid "contamination" by wearing gloves so that they will not feel compelled to wash. They may also seek reassurance that they have not touched "contaminated" objects.

Neuroleptic agents are rarely effective and should generally be avoided, because of the risk of tardive dyskinesia when these agents are used on a long-term basis. Short-term use of a benzodiazepine may be helpful during periods of intense anxiety; however, benzodiazepines do not appear to be effective in relieving obsessions and compulsions.

Approximately 80 percent of OCD patients who are treated with conventional pharmacologic therapies fail to improve significantly.[10]

Several controlled studies[5,9-15] have demonstrated that the investigational agents clomipramine (Anafranil®) and fluvoxamine — antidepressant medications with potent effects on serotonin neurotransmission — are effective in the treatment of OCD. Adequate doses (up to 250 mg/day for clomipramine and 300 mg/day for fluvoxamine) must be given for a sufficient length of time (at least six weeks) to achieve a reduction in symptoms. Fluoxetine (Prozac®), a new antidepressant that blocks serotonin reuptake, is also being studied in OCD.[16]

Studies have shown that as many as 80 percent of patients treated with clomipramine and fluvoxamine respond favorably, with an approximately 40 percent reduction in obsessions and rituals.[14,15] Although this may seem a modest improvement, patients and their physicians regard such a gain as notable.

MANAGEMENT

Because of the time consumed, interference with important activities, and distressful anxiety associated with OCD, most patients experience a secondary depression. Normally, however, this depression will resolve if the OCD responds to therapy. Severe depression can interfere with behavior therapy and may require treatment in its own right.

Approximately 25 percent of OCD patients either refuse behavior therapy or fail to comply with treatment instructions.[1] Family members are often cowed by the intensity of the patient's distress and demands for compliance with rituals. Like the patient, they may have forgotten how normal families function in matters of cleanliness, washing dishes and clothing, and so on. Verbal reassurance provided by family members with regard to obsessive worries may be particularly troublesome, actually undermining the effectiveness of both medications and behavior therapy. Patients can become "reassurance junkies" who feel better for a brief time when given a "fix" through their reassurance ritual (asking questions such as, "Did I wash after I went to the bathroom?" or "Did I touch the wastebasket when I walked past it?"). As with all addictions, the "fix" soon wears off and the urge for another fix of reassurance returns. Simply telling family members to stop reassuring the patient is seldom enough. Role-playing with family members, involving the use of neutral statements such as, "The doctor's instructions are that I am not to reassure," will help alleviate these patterns. Family therapy can be an important aid to recovery.

Although serious complications of pharmacologic treatment for OCD are rare, as many as 25 percent of patients will find the side effects so annoying that they will not be able to take these medications in therapeutic doses.[5,14] Patients with OCD may also abuse alcohol and/or antianxiety medications.

Psychosurgery is considered very rarely in severe, intractable cases of OCD after specialists have been consulted and all other treatments have failed to produce a significant response.

The symptoms of OCD may remit as the result of initial treatment, but some symptomatology usually persists. Through vigorous application of effective therapies, however, a substantial reduction in symptoms can usually be achieved. Once such improvement becomes evident, little management is needed to help patients maintain their gains. Behavior therapy, in particular, enables patients to treat new manifestations of OCD on their own. Ongoing pharmacologic treatment is the other cornerstone of continuing care.

TERMINATING THERAPY

After patients have learned to apply the techniques of exposure and response prevention successfully on their own, termination of treatment is appropriate. In those who are receiving pharmacologic therapy as well, monitoring by the physician can be done less frequently once the patient has achieved a stable, therapeutic dosage level deemed to provide maximal benefit.

SUPPORT GROUPS

Support groups for obsessive-compulsive

individuals and their families are often available in centers where large numbers of these patients are treated. Also, with growing awareness of the high prevalence of this disorder, more lay groups are being formed.

PATIENT EDUCATION

Information about OCD and its treatment is helpful to patients (see the patient information aid in the Appendix). Many of these individuals have felt alone with their disorder, and learning that others have very similar (and sometimes identical) obsessions and rituals reduces the fear of being "the only one." Information about available, effective treatments also provides hope of improvement. A useful aid for patients and families is *Obsessive-Compulsive Disorder: A Guide,*[7] which provides answers to questions commonly asked about the disorder and its treatment. *Anxiety and Its Treatment: Help Is Available*[6] contains a self-help behavior therapy section that has been found useful by some patients.

References

1. McDonald R, Marks IM, Blizard R: Quality control of outcome in mental health care: A model for routine use. *Health Trends,* in press.
2. Myers JK, Weissman MM, Tischler GL, et al: Six-month prevalence of psychiatric disorders in three communities. *Arch Gen Psychiatry* 1984;41:959-967.
3. Robins LN, Helzer JE, Weissman MM, et al: Lifetime prevalence of specific psychiatric disorders in three sites. *Arch Gen Psychiatry* 1984;41:949-958.
4. Baxter LR, Phelps ME, Mazziotta JC, et al: Local cerebral glucose metabolic rates in obsessive-compulsive disorder. *Arch Gen Psychiatry* 1987;44:211-218.
5. Marks IM, Lelliott P, Basoglu M, et al: Clomipramine, self-exposure and therapist-aided exposure for obsessive-compulsive rituals. *Br J Psychiatry* 1988;152:522-534.
6. Greist JH, Jefferson JW, Marks IM: *Anxiety and Its Treatment: Help Is Available.* Washington, DC, American Psychiatric Press, 1986.
7. Greist JH: *Obsessive-Compulsive Disorder: A Guide.* Madison, Wis, University of Wisconsin Board of Regents, 1988.
8. Marks IM: *Living With Fear.* New York, McGraw-Hill, 1978.
9. Marks IM, Stern RS, Mawson D, et al: Clomipramine and exposure for obsessive-compulsive rituals. *Br J Psychiatry* 1980;136:1-25.
10. Ananth J, Pecknold JC, Van Den Steen N, et al: Double-blind comparative study of clomipramine and amitriptyline in obsessive neurosis. *Prog Neuropsychopharmacol Biol Psychiatry* 1981; 5:257-262.
11. Thoren P, Asberg M, Cronholm B, et al: Clomipramine treatment of obsessive-compulsive disorder. *Arch Gen Psychiatry* 1980;37:1281-1285.
12. Insel TR, Murphy DL, Cohen RM, et al: Obsessive-compulsive disorder: A double-blind trial of clomipramine and clorgyline. *Arch Gen Psychiatry* 1983;40:605-612.
13. Price LH, Goodman WK, Charney DS, et al: Treatment of severe obsessive-compulsive disorder with fluvoxamine. *Am J Psychiatry* 1987;144:1059-1061.
14. Perse TL, Greist JH, Jefferson JW, et al: Fluvoxamine treatment of obsessive-compulsive disorder. *Am J Psychiatry* 1987;144:1543-1548.
15. Goodman WK, Price LH, Rasmussen SA, et al: Efficacy of fluvoxamine in obsessive-compulsive disorder: A double-blind comparison with placebo. *Arch Gen Psychiatry,* in press.
16. Fontaine R, Chouinard G: Fluoxetine in the treatment of obsessive-compulsive disorder. *Prog Neuropsychopharmacol Biol Psychiatry* 1985;9:605-608.

CLINICAL PRESENTATION

Panic disorder is characterized by *unexpected, unprovoked* attacks of cognitive and physical symptoms of anxiety. The attacks reach a symptomatic peak within 10 minutes of onset and taper off within 60 minutes. They occur, on average, two to four times per week. In a true panic attack, at least four of the characteristic symptoms are present.

Panic disorder is diagnosed in any patient who has *ever* had:

- four panic attacks within a four-week period; or
- one or more attacks followed by four weeks of continuous anticipatory anxiety about having another such attack.

Panic disorder can occur with or without agoraphobia. Most often, panic disorder occurs with agoraphobia. Agoraphobia without panic disorder is very rare.

In its natural history, panic disorder may progress through the following stages (although there are many variations):

Stage 1: Limited symptom attacks   **Stage 4:** Limited phobic avoidance
Stage 2: Panic attacks   **Stage 5:** Extensive phobic avoidance
Stage 3: Hypochondriasis   **Stage 6:** Secondary depression

The disorder may evolve rapidly—over days or weeks—or slowly—over months to years.

TREATMENT

Treatment of panic disorder is aimed at five targets:

- Controlling the biological component
- Patient education
- Extinguishing phobic avoidance behavior
- Eliminating any complicating psychosocial problems
- Long-term monitoring to prevent relapse

Nonpharmacologic Approaches

- Patient education
- Behavior therapy (i.e., in vivo exposure therapy) to treat phobic avoidance
- Psychotherapy, if obvious psychosocial problems are complicating recovery

Pharmacologic Approaches

Medications from the following drug classes have been studied in the treatment of panic disorder:

- Benzodiazepines
- Tricyclic antidepressants
- MAO inhibitors

CASE HISTORY

Maria R. is a 30-year-old physician who completed her residency two years ago. She gave birth to a baby girl six months ago. During maternity leave, she began to experience episodes of light-headedness and faintness. At other times, she felt her heart pounding and experienced occasional skipped beats. Several times a week she felt acutely short of breath, as if she couldn't get enough air into her lungs.

Believing that a postpartum anemia might explain her symptoms, she consulted a senior colleague, who found no evidence of anemia or other overt medical illness. He felt that her symptoms were probably related to the stress of her new responsibilities as a mother with a career. Maria remained puzzled and concerned, since her symptom attacks were often sudden and unprovoked, occurring even when she was not under stress. After an episode of paresthesias and numbness on the left side of her body, she consulted her textbooks in alarm, wondering if she might have early signs of a neurologic illness.

The week before consulting her primary care physician, Maria was overwhelmed by a symptomatic attack that occurred without warning while she was driving with her baby in the car. Things around her suddenly appeared strange, detached, and unfamiliar. Her heart pounded, she felt very faint and weak, and her legs and feet became so numb that it was difficult for her to drive. After that episode, she was afraid to drive with her baby, fearing that she would have another attack and lose control of the car.

Maria's primary care physician examined her and ordered routine laboratory evaluations; all the findings were within normal limits. Maria asked her physician to order an MRI scan and a complete endocrine workup. She was afraid of being perceived as a hypochondriac but felt certain that her worsening attacks had a physical basis.

After considerable reassurance by her physician, who was convinced that the correct diagnosis was panic disorder, Maria agreed to a trial of appropriate medication with close follow-up. Her symptoms improved promptly.

Panic disorder* is the most common of the severe anxiety disorders encountered in clinical practice. According to the latest diagnostic criteria,[1] panic disorder is present in many patients previously assumed to have generalized anxiety disorder. Panic disorder can occur with or without agoraphobia (fear of being in a place or a situation from which escape might be difficult or embarrassing, or in which help might not be available in the event of a panic attack); however, panic disorder with agoraphobia is much more common. Agoraphobia without panic disorder is very rare.

Since panic disorder is usually chronic and relapsing, and provokes a variety of somatic symptoms, patients may return to the primary care physician repeatedly for diagnostic evaluation and help in spite of prior assurances that "no medical illness is present." Costly and unnecessary evaluations and considerable frustration for both patient and physician have been frequent sequelae in the past. Fortunately, major advances have been made during the past decade in understanding the biological correlates and treatment of this common condition.[2-8,9-14]

CLINICAL PRESENTATION

Panic disorder is characterized by *unexpected, unprovoked* attacks of cognitive symptoms (dread, fear) and physical symptoms (palpitations, trembling, shortness of breath) of anxiety. (A characteristic case is described in the Case History.) The attacks have a rapid onset; the surge of symptoms is sudden, reaching a peak within 10 minutes and tapering off within 60 minutes. The typical patient has two to four attacks per week, often complicated by anticipatory anxiety as well as one or more phobias associated with various environmental stimuli—e.g., crowds, highways, being far from home. Clinically, the diagnostic focus should be on eliciting the unexpected nature of at least some of the attacks.[4-8]

A panic attack is defined not by the intensity of the anxiety experience, but by the number of symptoms.[1] In a true panic attack, at least four of the 13 characteristic symptoms (see Table 1) must be present. An episode associated with fewer than four symptoms is called a "limited symp-

---

*Paroxysmal anxiety disorder, ICD-10 draft, 1987

Table 1
Diagnostic Criteria for Panic Disorder

A. At some time during the disturbance, one or more panic attacks have occurred that were unexpected and not triggered by situations in which the person was the focus of others' attention.

B. Either four attacks have occurred within a four-week period, or one or more attacks have been followed by a period of at least a month of persistent fear of having another attack.

C. At least four of the following symptoms occurred during at least one of the attacks:

    (1) shortness of breath (dyspnea) or smothering sensations
    (2) dizziness, unsteady feelings, or faintness
    (3) palpitations or accelerated heart rate (tachycardia)
    (4) trembling or shaking
    (5) sweating
    (6) choking
    (7) nausea or abdominal distress
    (8) depersonalization or derealization
    (9) numbness or tingling sensations (paresthesias)
    (10) flushes (hot flashes) or chills
    (11) chest pain or discomfort
    (12) fear of dying
    (13) fear of going crazy or of doing something uncontrolled

D. During at least some of the attacks, at least four of the symptoms developed suddenly and increased in intensity within 10 minutes of the beginning of the first symptom noticed in the attack.

E. No organic factor (e.g., amphetamine or caffeine intoxication, hyperthyroidism) initiated and maintained the disturbance.

Adapted with permission from *DSM-III-R*.[1]

tom attack." Thus, an intense feeling of panic accompanied only by tachycardia is *not* defined as a panic attack. However, an episode of tachycardia plus shortness of breath, light-headedness, and paresthesias in association with anxiety feelings *is* a panic attack, even if the anxiety is not intense enough for the patient to characterize it as "panic."

Any patient who has *ever* had four panic attacks within a four-week period, or one or more attacks followed by four weeks of continuous anticipatory anxiety over having another attack, is given the diagnosis of panic disorder.[1] Even if the attack or cluster of attacks occurred quite some time ago and the patient's current anxiety level is milder by comparison, the diagnosis is still panic disorder.

The typical symptoms that occur during panic attacks (Table 1) are familiar to virtually every primary care physician. However, different symptoms may predominate in different patients. For example, one patient may complain primarily of a skipping, pounding, and racing heartbeat and shortness of breath, while another may have attacks of diarrhea, light-headedness, and imbalance. Over time, most patients with panic disorder will experience the majority of the characteristic symptoms.

In its natural history, panic disorder may progress through the following stages[5,8] (although there are many variations):

Stage 1: Limited symptom attacks
Stage 2: Panic attacks
Stage 3: Hypochondriasis
Stage 4: Limited phobic avoidance
Stage 5: Extensive phobic avoidance
Stage 6: Secondary depression

The disorder may evolve rapidly—over days or weeks—or slowly—over months or years.

The patient with panic disorder may initially present during any of the typical stages, and the physician may be tempted to elevate the present clinical picture into a diagnostic entity unto itself by labeling the patient with a diagnosis of the moment (such as Meniere's disease or simple phobia). However, these presentations may not be separate entities, but rather different stages of the same disorder.[5] Many patients with panic disorder have a history of multiple nonspecific diagnoses, such as labyrinthitis, mitral valve prolapse, hyperventilation syndrome, hypoglycemia, supraventricular tachycardia, irritable colon, and premenstrual syndrome,[4-7,15,16] as a result of having had the dominant symptom viewed in isolation. The best way to ensure diagnostic accuracy is to adopt a longitudinal perspective and an integrated view of panic disorder as a *single evolving process.*

Approximately half of all cases start at Stage 1 (the other half start at Stage 2) with attacks of one or two somatic symptoms with or without cognitive anxiety. Eventually, several symptoms occur together, accompanied by significant cognitive alarm (i.e., a true panic attack). If the physician diagnoses panic disorder correctly at an early stage, the patient will be less likely to progress to the later, more disabling stages of the illness.

When at a loss to find a stress-related reason for the unexpected anxiety attacks, the patient with panic disorder often concludes that a serious medical illness must be present. This conviction often persists in spite of medical assurances to the contrary. At this stage, patients may be labeled hypochondriacs as they become preoccupied by and fear their bodily responses.

As panic attacks continue, they may become associated in the patient's mind with various environmental stimuli, which now become conditioned phobic cues. Over time, phobic avoidance behavior may progressively worsen to the point of agoraphobia (which literally means fear of the marketplace or of places where people assemble, but also describes any extensive phobic avoidance behavior). Some patients may even become housebound. Eventually, many patients develop secondary depression due to the progressive disability and demoralization caused by panic disorder.

If the unexpected anxiety attacks are frequent and intense, the patient can progress rapidly through all of the stages. If the attacks become milder, the patient may remain at the existing stage and not progress further until the attacks again increase in frequency or severity. In about 15 percent of cases, the attacks stop entirely, with complete remission of symptoms.[17,18]

EPIDEMIOLOGY

The Epidemiologic Catchment Area survey found that 1.5 percent of the adult population had panic disorder.[19] This is certainly an underestimate; using the current (*DSM-III-R*) broadened criteria for panic disorder, the lifetime prevalence would probably be 3 or 4 percent of the adult population. Panic disorder has a uniform unimodal age-of-onset distribution, with a peak in the 20s.[20] It rarely begins before the age of 12 or after the age of 40. In the over-65 age group,[19] it is present only about $\frac{1}{12}$ as often as in the 25-to-44 age group.[19] Approximately 75 percent of patients with panic disorder are women.[7,19]

ETIOLOGY

Panic disorder is the product of three forces—psychological, behavioral, and biological. It may be complicated by acquired phobias and, like virtually any other illness, it may be aggravated by stress and conflict. However, the past decade has witnessed a dramatic shift in focus toward a biological view of panic disorder. It is now believed that panic disorder is a genetically influenced disease similar to other metabolic diseases and that biological factors are an important part of the disorder.[4,6,8-14,21,22]

Several specific biological correlates of panic disorder have been proposed involving the following areas of the brain: the locus ceruleus,[11] the GABA/benzodiazepine receptor complex,[12,14] the septo-hippocampal region,[9,13] and the ventro-medullary center.[10]

The locus ceruleus is a small nucleus in the pons of the brain stem, containing about 50 percent of all the noradrenergic neurons in the central nervous system. Its primary neurotransmitter is norepinephrine. Stimulation of the locus ceruleus results in sympathetic arousal and an outpouring of catecholamines, which leads to the symptomatic expression of the illness.[11]

Gamma-aminobutyric acid (GABA) is the brain's major inhibitory neurotransmitter. It opens up ion channels in neuronal membranes, causing hyperpolarization of the neurons and decreasing their excitability. This results in a decrease in anxiety.[12,14] Various compounds are capable of acting at receptor sites that are closely associated with the GABA receptors. Some of these compounds (e.g., the benzodiazepines) enhance the action of GABA and calm anxiety. Others have an opposite, anxiety-activating, effect.

The septo-hippocampal region of the

brain matches and compares input information from the environment, from the body, and from memory. When it detects a mismatch, it intervenes by inhibiting behavior.[9] Panic disorder may involve a hypersensitivity of this region. In recent positron emission tomography (PET) scan studies of patients with panic disorder, an asymmetry in blood flow was noted between the right and left parahippocampal gyri.[13]

Intravenous infusions of a half-molar solution of sodium lactate will precipitate panic attacks in patients with panic disorder.[4] Yet sodium lactate does not cross the blood-brain barrier to any great extent. Thus, investigators have wondered how it can provoke such an apparently central response. One possible explanation involves the ventromedullary center, one of the few parts of the brain without a significant blood-brain barrier. Its function is to respond to pCO_2, pH, and lactate alterations in the blood by causing central nervous system arousal. It has been proposed that the chemoceptors in this region are hypersensitive in patients with panic disorder, responding with greater intensity to lower threshold levels of CO_2 and lactate.[10]

Studies have found evidence of vertical transmission from generation to generation,[23] as well as greater concordance in monozygotic than in dizygotic twins.[22] The transmission pattern within families is consistent with single-locus genetics, and preliminary findings implicate the long arm of chromosome 16.[21]

These correlates are probably parts of a much larger puzzle that will be unraveled more fully in the future.

TREATMENT

Treatment of the typical patient with panic disorder should be aimed at five targets:

1. Controlling the biological part of the disorder
2. Patient education
3. Extinguishing phobic avoidance behavior
4. Eliminating any complicating psychosocial problems
5. Long-term monitoring to prevent relapse.

Focusing exclusively on any one target is likely to result in an incomplete response; however, not every patient will need or benefit from all five steps. Patients with limited symptom attacks may require only an accurate diagnosis, some patient education, and close follow-up. Patient education is an essential part of treatment for any patient with panic disorder (see the patient information aid in the Appendix). Part of the patient education process is to make the patient aware that medication is available to treat the disorder and alleviate symptoms. Some patients are unwilling to take medication and may prefer to do without it. In most severe cases, however, pharmacologic treatment makes a great contribution to a successful outcome.

In deciding whether or not to treat the patient pharmacologically, the physician should consider:

- the frequency of the attacks
- the patient's attitude toward taking medication
- the severity of the attacks
- the amount of social disability or lifestyle disruption
- any history of drug abuse.

When the patient is seen on follow-up, the physician should look for signs of continuing disability, such as increased self-medication with alcohol, increased time away from work, increased preoccupation with symptoms, and persistent discomfort.[24] If these signs occur, pharmacologic intervention should be considered.

Nonpharmacologic Approaches

Patient education. Explaining the disorder to the patient and reassuring the patient that effective treatment is available are the first steps in the educational process. Patients need to know that their symptom patterns are characteristic of the disorder and that the disorder has biochemical and genetic correlates.

The physician may have to spend a significant amount of time undoing the harm of previous false labeling. Patients may have been told that the symptoms were "all in the head" or secondary to an organic disease such as mitral valve prolapse or premenstrual syndrome.

An important part of patient education is involving a "significant other," whenever possible, in any treatment discussions. The support of the patient's family can be invaluable—especially in the first month or so of treatment, when medication side effects may be more prominent than the benefits. Patients *and* families should know that panic disorder is a real illness—*not* a weakness of character—and that medication is *not* a "crutch" but a means of correcting a real biological abnormality.[6,8,21]

Behavior therapy. Any event can become associated in the mind with a specific response; thus, any situation in which a panic attack occurs can acquire the ability to elicit a fear reaction on its own. For example, if a panic attack occurs in an elevator, the patient may begin to fear elevators. Usually, this sort of association must occur repeatedly before a phobia is established. However, when a spontaneous panic attack is particularly severe, a new phobia may be created immediately. Over time, as panic attacks occur in a variety of settings, the number of phobias may increase, anticipatory anxiety feelings may worsen, and the patient may become more disabled.

After a patient has been symptom-free for several weeks, the physician might encourage the patient to encounter intentionally the phobic stimuli. With a little practice, many patients eventually feel comfortable in the previously avoided situations.[17,25-28]

When phobias are long-standing and severe, however, more formal behavior therapy may be required. Many types of behavior therapy have been used in treating phobias, but all have one common ingredient: real-life exposure to the phobic stimulus.[25,27-30]

Duration of exposure is probably the most important factor in the success of this treatment.[26-30] Exposure sessions lasting two to three hours are superior to those lasting less than one hour. Other factors enhancing success include frequent repetition of exposure sessions, preventing the patient from making his or her usual avoidance response, and structuring the sessions to be as true-to-life as possible.[27-30]

With the help of medication, many patients are pleasantly surprised at the ease and speed with which they overcome their phobias with in vivo exposure. Nevertheless, an occasional patient remains too frightened even to begin to participate in exposure therapy.

Psychotherapy. There is no evidence that psychotherapy, when used alone, is any more effective than placebo in the treatment of patients with panic disorder. The response rate to psychotherapy alone is about 13 percent.[6] However, if the patient has psychosocial problems complicating recovery, formal psychotherapy may mean the difference between a partial and a complete response. The psychotherapeutic approach can range from informal counseling to in-depth treatment. In many cases, the primary care physician's relationship with the patient is a powerful psychological tool on its own.

Pharmacologic Approaches
Several classes of medications have been studied in the treatment of panic disorder. These include benzodiazepines such as alprazolam (Xanax®)[5,8,31-37] and clonazepam (Klonopin®)[38-41]; tricyclic antidepressants such as imipramine (Tofranil®)[2-8,28,35,42] and desipramine (Norpramin®, Pertofrane®),[43,44] and monoamine oxidase (MAO) inhibitors such as phenelzine (Nardil®).[45] Other agents under study show promise.

All of these medications appear to be equally effective in treating mild and early cases of panic disorder. Alprazolam, the best-studied benzodiazepine in the treatment of panic disorder, appears to be the least toxic and most rapidly effective.[5] Phenelzine may be the most effective in severe, chronic cases,[7] but it requires strict avoidance of certain foods and of common prescription and nonprescription drugs[7,45]; therefore, it is usually reserved for use in patients who have not responded to benzodiazepines or tricyclic antidepressants.

With all the medications, the most common reason for treatment failure is use of inadequate doses for inadequate lengths of time. Careful adjustment of dosage over time can make a difference between a mediocre and a superior result; in fact, these medications should be titrated and adjusted with as much care as is usually devoted to the prescribing of insulin for diabetic patients. The best way to strike a balance between side effects and benefits is to review closely dosage schedules and timing of doses in relation to panic attacks. In many cases, optimal results seem to coincide with the presence of a low level of the side effects typically associated with the given medication.

The initial dosage of any medication for panic disorder should be low, then gradually increased over several weeks to minimize side effects and keep pace with the inevitable tolerance that develops. If the dosage is not increased appropriately, the patient is unlikely to benefit at all or may lose any initial improvement within a few weeks. A patient may go through two or three plateaus of tolerance before reaching the final effective dose—often after three months. During that time, therefore, the need to increase dosage does *not* indicate that the patient is becoming "addicted" or is a potential drug abuser. Fortunately, tolerance to side effects often develops more rapidly than does tolerance to beneficial effects.[46,47]

The usual maximum daily dosage of alprazolam is 4 mg; however, final doses of 6 mg/day or more have been used successfully in the treatment of panic disorder.[5] With tricyclics, the usual final effective dosage is at least 150 mg/day, and the average patient requires 200 mg/day.[28] With the MAO inhibitor phenelzine, 45 to 60 mg/day usually controls panic disorder.[45]

Alprazolam often begins to work within the first several days of treatment.[5] Medications in other classes take four to six weeks, on average, to produce stable clinical benefits. In a few patients, an initial beneficial response may appear even later.[2-5,7]

LONG-TERM MANAGEMENT

Duration of pharmacologic treatment, and dosage, should be carefully individualized. In most cases of panic disorder, medication should be continued for six to 12 months.[5,6] Then, if the patient has remained symptom-free for an extended period, the medication can be slowly tapered over two or three months. Within three months of completely discontinuing medication, however, more than 70 percent of patients experience some recurrence of symptoms. Many—perhaps most—patients will need medication for years if they are to remain free of disability.

The majority of patients with panic disorder have a chronic fluctuating course for the better part of their adult lives. As many as 50 percent or more have some degree of disability, and 73 to 94 percent are symptomatic when reevaluated up to 20 years after initial diagnosis.[6,17,18,48] Compared with controls matched for age and sex, patients with panic disorder have higher mortality rates from suicide and, among males, from cardiovascular disease.[18,49]

Ultimately, patient education is one of the most powerful tools for ensuring a long-term favorable outcome. Patients who have a good understanding of their disorder are much more likely to comply with treatment, to detect relapses accurately and deal with them appropriately, to report symptoms accurately, thus facilitating pharmacologic adjustment, and to maintain a positive self-image, putting their disorder in its proper perspective in their lives.

Support groups for patients with panic disorder or agoraphobia are now common in many communities. They can be of immense benefit in a number of ways: They provide support, encouragement, and education, and they give patients the opportunity to see firsthand that they are not alone and that many people have recovered successfully.

WHEN TO REFER

The primary care physician is often the first medical contact for the patient with panic disorder and can probably manage the majority of cases successfully. However, if a patient has failed to respond to pharmacologic treatment at adequate dosage levels continued for an adequate length of time, then referral to a psychiatrist skillful in psychopharmacology is recommended. When formal in vivo exposure therapy is needed to deal with phobic avoidance behavior, referral to a therapist skilled in these techniques is indicated.

In actual practice, only a small number of cases will need to be referred. With careful attention to the details outlined above, the primary care physician should find that most patients with panic disorder are rewarding to treat and can be managed quite successfully in the primary care setting.

References

1. American Psychiatric Association: *Diagnostic and Statistical Manual of Mental Disorders*, Third Edition—Revised. Washington, DC, American Psychiatric Association, 1987.
2. Klein DF: Delineation of two drug-responsive anxiety syndromes. *Psychopharmacologia* 1964;5:397-408.
3. Klein DF: Importance of psychiatric diagnosis and prediction of clinical drug effects. *Arch Gen Psychiatry* 1967;16:118-126.
4. Klein DF, Rabkin JG: Anxiety: New research and changing concepts. New York, Raven Press, 1981.
5. Sheehan DV: Current perspectives in the treatment of panic and phobic disorders.

Drug Ther 1982;12(9):179-193.

6. Sheehan DV: Panic attacks and phobias. *New Engl J Med* 1982;307:156-158.

7. Sheehan DV, Ballenger J, Jacobson G: Treatment of endogenous anxiety with phobic, hysterical, and hypochondriacal symptoms. *Arch Gen Psychiatry* 1980; 31:51-59.

8. Sheehan DV: *The Anxiety Disease.* New York, E Scribner & Sons, 1983 (revised paperback edition, New York, Bantam Books, 1986).

9. Gray JA: *The Neuropsychology of Anxiety: An Inquiry into the Functions of the Septo-hippocampal System.* Oxford, Oxford University Press, 1982.

10. Carr DB, Sheehan DV: Panic anxiety: A new biological model. *J Clin Psychiatry* 1984;45(8):323-330.

11. Redmond DE: Alterations in the function of the nucleus locus coeruleus: A possible model of four studies of anxiety, in Hanin I, Usdin E (eds): *Animal Models in Psychiatry and Neurology.* New York, Pergamon Press, 1987.

12. Paul SM, Skolnick P: Benzodiazepine receptors and psychopathological states: Towards the neurobiology of anxiety, in Klein DF, Rabkin JG (eds): *Anxiety: New Research and Changing Concepts.* New York, Raven Press, 1981.

13. Reiman EM, Raichle ME, Butler FK, et al: PET focal brain abnormality in panic disorder. *Nature* 1984;310:683-685.

14. Insel TR, Ninan PT, Aloy J, et al: A benzodiazepine receptor mediated model of anxiety: Studies in non-human primates and clinical implications. *Arch Gen Psychiatry* 1984;41:741-750.

15. Fishman SM, Sheehan DV, Carr DB: Thyroid indices in panic disorder. *J Clin Psychiatry* 1985;46:422-423.

16. Liberthson R, Sheehan DV, King ME, et al: The prevalence of mitral valve prolapse in patients with panic disorders. *Am J Psychiatry* 1986;143:511-515.

17. Marks IM, Lader M: Anxiety states (anxiety neurosis): A review. *J Nerv Ment Dis* 1973;156:3-18.

18. Noyes R, Clancy J, Hoenk PR, et al: The prognosis of anxiety neurosis. *Arch Gen Psychiatry* 1980; 37:173-178.

19. Robins LN, Helzer JE, Weissman MM, et al: Lifetime prevalence of specific psychiatric disorders in three sites. *Arch Gen Psychiatry* 1984;41:949-958.

20. Sheehan DV, Sheehan KE, Minichiello WE: Age of onset of phobic disorders: A reevaluation. *Compr Psychiatry* 1981; 22:544-553.

21. Crowe RR, Noyes R Jr, Wilson AF, et al: A linkage study of panic disorder. *Arch Gen Psychiatry* 1987;44:933-937.

22. Torgersen S: Genetic factors in anxiety disorders. *Arch Gen Psychiatry* 1983; 40;1085-1089.

23. Pauls DL, Bucher KD, Crowe RR, et al: A genetic study of panic disorder pedigrees. *Am J Hum Genet* 1980;32:639-644.

24. Bibb JL, Chambless DL: Alcohol use and abuse among diagnosed agoraphobics. *Behav Res Ther* 1986;24:49-58.

25. Marks IM: *Fears, Phobias and Rituals.* New York, Oxford University Press, 1987.

26. Marks IM: *Fears and Phobias.* New York, Academic Press, 1969.

27. Telch MJ, Agras WS, Taylor CB, et al: Combined pharmacological and behavioral treatment for agoraphobia. *Behav Res Ther* 1985;23:325-355.

28. Mavissakalian M, Michelson L: Two-year follow-up of exposure and imipramine treatment of agoraphobia. *Am J Psychiatry* 1986;143:1106-1112.

29. Marks IM: The current status of behavioral psychotherapy: Theory and practice. *Am J Psychiatry* 1976;133:253-261.

30. Sherman AR: Real-life exposure as a primary therapeutic factor in the desensitization treatment of fear. *J Abnorm Psychol* 1972;79:19-28.

31. Chouinard G, Annable L, Fontaine R, et al: Alprazolam in the treatment of generalized anxiety and panic disorders: A double-blind, placebo-controlled study. *Psychopharmacology* 1982;77:229-233.

32. Sheehan DV, Claycomb JB, Surman OS: The relative efficacy of phenelzine, imipramine, alprazolam, and placebo in the treatment of panic attacks and agoraphobia. Presented at meeting on Biology of Panic Disorders, Boston, November 5, 1983.

33. Sheehan, DV, Coleman JH, Greenblatt DJ, et al: Some biochemical correlates of panic attacks with agoraphobia and their response to a new treatment. *J Clin Psychopharmacol* 1984;4:66-75.

34. Alexander PE, Alexander DD: Alprazolam treatment for panic disorders. *J Clin Psychiatry* 1986;47:301-304.

35. Charney DS, Woods SW, Goodman WK, et al: Drug treatment of panic disorder: The comparative efficacy of imipramine, alprazolam, and trazodone. *J Clin Psychiatry* 1986;47:580-586.

36. Carr D, Sheehan DV, Surman OS, et al: Neuroendocrine correlates of lactate-induced anxiety and their response to chronic alprazolam therapy. *Am J Psychiatry* 1986;143:483-494.

37. Ballenger JC, Burrows GD, DuPont R, et al: Alprazolam in panic disorder and agoraphobia: Results from a multicenter trial: I. Efficacy in short-term treatment. *Arch Gen Psychiatry* 1988;45:413-422.

38. Fontaine R, Chouinard G: Antipanic effect of clonazepam. *Am J Psychiatry* 1984;141:149.

39. Fontaine R: Clonazepam for panic disorders and agitation. *Psychosomatics* 1985;26(12 suppl):13-18.

40. Tesar GE, Rosenbaum JF, Pollack MH, et al: Clonazepam versus alprazolam in the treatment of panic disorder: Interim analysis of data from a prospective, double-blind, placebo-controlled trial. *J Clin Psychiatry* 1987;48(suppl):16-19.

41. Pollack MH, Rosenbaum JF, Tesar GE, et al: Clonazepam in the treatment of panic disorder and agoraphobia. *Psychopharmacol Bull* 1987;23:141-144.

42. Zitrin CM, Klein DF, Woerner MG, et al: Treatment of phobias. I. Comparison of imipramine hydrochloride and placebo. *Arch Gen Psychiatry* 1983;40:125-138.

43. Muskin PR, Fyer AJ: Treatment of panic disorder. *J Clin Psychopharmacol* 1981; 1:81-90.

44. Liebowitz MR, Fyer AJ, Gorman JM, et al: Lactate provocation of panic attacks: I. Clinical and behavioral findings. *Arch Gen Psychiatry* 1984;13:764-770.

45. Sheehan DV, Claycomb JB, Kouretas N: MAO inhibitors: Prescription and patient management. *Int J Psychiatry Med* 1980; 10:99-121.

46. Rickels K, Case WG, Downing RW, et al: Long-term diazepam therapy and clinical outcome. *JAMA* 1983;250:767-771.

47. Uhlenhuth EH, DeWit H, Balter MB, et al: Risks and benefits of long-term benzodiazepine use. *J Clin Psychopharmacol* 1988;8:161-167.

48. Wheeler EO, White PD, Reed EW, et al: Neurocirculatory asthenia (anxiety neurosis, effort syndrome, neurasthenia). A 20-year follow-up study of 173 patients. *JAMA* 1950;142:878-889.

49. Coryell W, Noyes R, Clancy J: Excess mortality in panic disorder. *Arch Gen Psychiatry* 1982;39:701-703.

CLINICAL PRESENTATION

Posttraumatic stress disorder (PTSD) can occur following a traumatic event that is outside the range of normal human experience (such as an accident, natural disaster, assault, rape, incest, combat, or kidnapping). The patient may have either been the direct victim of the trauma or witnessed it. Patients exhibit at least one symptom indicating persistent reexperiencing of the trauma and display at least three symptoms of persistent avoidance of stimuli associated with the trauma or a numbing of general responsiveness. In addition, they have at least two persistent symptoms of increased arousal since the time of the trauma and have experienced these symptoms for at least one month. Symptoms include:

- Sleep disturbance
- Social withdrawal or distancing
- Behavioral change, including outbursts, irritability, or physical abusiveness
- Alcohol or drug abuse
- Antisocial behavior or violation of the law
- Depression or suicidal ideas or attempts
- High levels of anxious arousal or psychological instability
- Nonspecific somatic complaints (e.g., headache)

TREATMENT

Because of the difference in recommended treatment approaches, it is essential to distinguish between acute and chronic PTSD.

Nonpharmacologic Approaches

- Psychotherapy
- Support groups
- Family counseling
- Relaxation techniques or biofeedback
- Referral of the patient to vocational rehabilitation services, if necessary
- Frequent visits with the primary care physician

Pharmacologic Approaches

- Tricyclic antidepressants, monoamine oxidase (MAO) inhibitors, and benzodiazepines have been used in both acute and chronic PTSD.
- Lithium, carbamazepine, neuroleptic agents, beta blockers, and clonidine have been used in selected cases of chronic PTSD.

CASE HISTORY 1

Molly G., a 62-year-old widowed white woman, presented to her primary care physician with complaints of extreme social withdrawal, tearfulness, suicidal rumination, headache, irritability, insomnia, and incessant thoughts of a recent near-death experience. Employed as a bookkeeper in a small business, she had not been able to work for the past week.

Molly was discharged recently from the hospital after an almost tragic error was made in her treatment. She had suffered from asthma since childhood, and shortly before admission had experienced a severe episode that could not be alleviated by outpatient therapy. She was admitted, and IV medications were ordered but she did not respond. Twelve hours later she began experiencing increasing chest pain and severe shortness of breath, and was rushed to the coronary care unit. Blood studies revealed no drug levels in her serum. It was learned that the nurse had neglected to add the prescribed medication to the IV solution.

Molly was later informed by her physician that she had almost died. She was treated, gradually responded, and was able to return home in one week. Molly told her daughter that she "was supposed to die," thought she had died, and wanted "to join Abe" (her deceased husband).

Because of the characteristic features of sleep disturbance, social withdrawal, behavioral change, hypervigilance, suicidal ideation, and nonspecific somatic complaints, the physician made a diagnosis of *acute* posttraumatic stress disorder. He prescribed a low-dose, short-term regimen of a sedating benzodiazepine to be taken at bedtime for Molly's insomnia. After discussion of several treatment alternatives, Molly decided to see the therapist at the local mental health center who had counseled her two years earlier when her husband died. Molly recovered gradually over a six-month period of psychotherapy. Her family consulted an attorney, and a lawsuit was filed against the hospital.

Four years later, the physician's records were subpoenaed. Careful notations in the medical record were helpful in substantiating Molly's account of the trauma and its aftermath.

Posttraumatic stress disorder (PTSD) follows the occurrence of a traumatic event that is outside the range of normal human experience and that would be considered distressing by almost anybody. The event usually involves some threat to life or safety, such as an accident, natural disaster, assault, rape, incest, combat, unexpected loss of home or property, or kidnapping. A patient may have been either the direct victim of the trauma or involved as an onlooker in witnessing the death, injury, or abuse of another person.

In arriving at a judgment as to whether or not the event was traumatic, the physician must explore the significance with which the patient views the event. Some events that ultimately were not life threatening could still be perceived by the patient as having been traumatic at the time.[1] The physician should also investigate preceding events that may have been more traumatic for the patient, as well as look for earlier episodes suggesting other mental disorders.

The diagnostic criteria for PTSD are shown in Table 1.[2] Note that in order to qualify for the diagnosis, the patient must exhibit at least one symptom indicating persistent reexperiencing of the trauma, display at least three symptoms of persistent avoidance of stimuli associated with the trauma or a numbing of general responsiveness, and have at least two persistent symptoms of increased arousal since the time of the trauma.

In addition, the patient's symptoms must have continued for at least one month. If at least six months have passed between the occurrence of the trauma and the development of the symptoms, the patient is considered to have delayed PTSD.

It is important for the physician to understand that patients with PTSD will not always present by describing the above symptoms as the primary complaint. Even if patients do so, it is unusual for them to have drawn a connection between the symptoms and a previous trauma. Feelings of shame, guilt, a tendency to repress unpleasant events, and/or insufficient awareness may all conspire to an initial concealment of traumatic events.

It is also important to keep good records. Because litigation is common in cases of PTSD, the primary care physician should consider the possibility of having to testify regarding the opinions and findings noted in the patient's record.

CASE HISTORY 2

Steve W., a 40-year-old white man, presented to his primary care physician seeking narcotics for chronic pain ("I was shot in the war and never really healed") and a tranquilizer for "shot nerves." He complained of chronic headaches and leg pain, and said that his arms "get paralyzed." He answered three of the CAGE questions on alcoholism positively. He denied drug use or abuse and appeared restless and hostile ("*You* aren't going to help me, either"). He reported nightmares, early-morning awakening, and loss of interest in pleasurable activities but denied suicidal ideation or anorexia.

Steve is the son of a successful businessman and a teacher. He was valedictorian of his high school class and married his high school sweetheart. Steve spent four years in Vietnam, was wounded twice, saw heavy combat regularly, and was well decorated. He has been married twice, is now separated, and has three children (one from his first marriage, two from his second). He has lost every job he has held due to his habitual outbursts of anger and has been jailed four times for minor offenses (e.g., being abusive to a police officer). Although he was graduated from the local community college with a degree in computer science, he has not applied his training. He has spent the past two years living alone in the woods.

Steve's physician made a diagnosis of *chronic* posttraumatic stress disorder and alcohol abuse. He referred Steve to a local veterans support group and to Alcoholics Anonymous. Steve's wife and children received counseling aimed at educating them about Steve's disorders.

Once Steve's physician was sure that Steve had stopped drinking, he started him on a low dose of desipramine, increasing to 200 mg/day, which markedly lessened his pain, sleep disturbance, and agitation. Steve was referred to the local Office of Vocational Rehabilitation. He began working at a computer store and eventually was able to move back home with his wife and children.

CLINICAL PRESENTATION

Once PTSD has been suspected, the physician must ask tactfully and empathically about the occurrence of past traumatic events. When this topic is first approached, the patient may show an affective response that conveys at least as much as the verbal response. This affect may consist of a growing tearfulness, a quiet introspective feeling of shame with avoidance of eye contact, or anger, agitation, or hostility. Common presentations include the following:

- **Sleep disturbance.** Any patient presenting with sleep disturbance should be asked about nightmares. Because nightmares associated with PTSD characteristically depict actual life events in graphic detail, any individual describing unusually vivid or lifelike nightmares should be suspected of having the disorder. The patient may awaken sweating or agitated, perhaps shouting or otherwise vocalizing, as well as grabbing or assaulting the sleeping partner.

- **Social withdrawal, distancing, and alienation from others, including significant family members.** Behavior of this kind, when not in keeping with the previous personality, should prompt a suspicion of PTSD.

- **Behavioral change, with explosive outbursts, irritability, or physical abusiveness toward other people.**

- **Abuse of alcohol or drugs, especially if used to deaden some painful experience, memory, or affect.**

- **Antisocial behavior or violation of the law.** If such behavior was absent during adolescence, a diagnosis of PTSD should be considered.

- **Depression or suicidal ideas or attempts.**

- **High levels of anxious arousal or physiologic instability.**

- **Nonspecific somatic complaints** (e.g., headache).

EPIDEMIOLOGY

PTSD is not a rare condition; the lifetime prevalence is approximately 1 percent, and 15 percent of the general population may experience some of its symptoms after severe trauma (such as physical at-

Table 1
Diagnostic Criteria for Posttraumatic Stress Disorder

A. The person has experienced an event that is outside the range of usual human experience and that would be markedly distressing to almost anyone, e.g., serious threat to one's life or physical integrity; harm to one's children, spouse, close relatives, or friends; sudden destruction of one's home or community; or seeing another person who has recently been, or is being, seriously injured or killed.

B. The traumatic event is persistently reexperienced in at least one of the following ways:

   (1) recurrent and intrusive distressing recollections of the event
   (2) recurrent distressing dreams of the event
   (3) sudden acting or feeling as if the traumatic event were recurring
   (4) intense psychological distress at exposure to events that symbolize or resemble an aspect of the traumatic event, including anniversaries of the trauma

C. Persistent avoidance of stimuli associated with the trauma or numbing of general responsiveness (not present before the trauma), as indicated by at least three of the following:

   (1) efforts to avoid thoughts or feelings associated with the trauma
   (2) efforts to avoid activities or situations that arouse recollections of the trauma
   (3) inability to recall an important aspect of the trauma (psychogenic amnesia)
   (4) markedly diminished interest in significant activities
   (5) feeling of detachment or estrangement from others
   (6) restricted range of affect
   (7) sense of a foreshortened future

D. Persistent symptoms of increased arousal, as indicated by at least two of the following:

   (1) difficulty falling or staying asleep
   (2) irritability or outbursts of anger
   (3) difficulty concentrating
   (4) hypervigilance
   (5) exaggerated startle response
   (6) physiologic reactivity upon exposure to events that symbolize or resemble an aspect of the traumatic event

E. Duration of the disturbance (symptoms in B, C, and D) of at least one month. Specify delayed onset if the onset of symptoms was at least six months after the trauma.

Adapted with permission from *DSM-III-R.*[2]

tack or combat).[3] PTSD becomes chronic in a significant number of individuals. In the community, it is frequently associated with other mental illnesses including affective disorders and abuse of alcohol and other drugs (Davidson JRT, Hughes D, Blazer DG, et al, unpublished data).

ETIOLOGY

If a diagnosis of PTSD is suspected, the physician should explore the etiology of PTSD from three perspectives: pretrauma, peritrauma, and posttrauma characteristics. A series of interviews may be required to elicit this information.

Important pretrauma risk factors include traits such as dependency, borderline personality characteristics, or sociopathic behavior, all of which impair an individual's ability to cope with traumatic stress. The occurrence of earlier trauma (e.g., childhood abuse, incest, previous accident) may increase the risk that a later traumatic event could lead to PTSD. A history of a chaotic childhood and family psychopathology also confers risk. In addition, the age of the patient should be considered, because the very young and very old have more difficulty coping with extreme stress. Previous mental illness confers additional risk. Protective factors, on the other hand, include the patient's ability to maintain emotional control, the presence of good self-esteem, the ability to achieve meaningful integration of the traumatic experience into the person's life at the time, and the presence of good social support.[4-6]

Peritrauma characteristics (the nature of the trauma itself) may determine outcome. Thus, trauma persisting for a long time (e.g., incest, child abuse, captivity, or combat) may induce a more enduring response than would a trauma of very brief duration. Whether the trauma is man made or an "act of God" can determine both the likelihood and characteristics of PTSD. Man-made traumata are often associated with greater feelings of distrust, bitterness, vengefulness, and litigiousness. If the patient was isolated at the time of the trauma, the risk of PTSD is also increased.[6]

Response to trauma is also related to posttrauma factors, such as the availability of support systems and trusted confidants; that may be one reason why loss of family and/or community is so devastating for trauma victims. The early availability of help is important and influences the outcome. The response of the family should be addressed, because relatives who promote dependent behavior on the part of the patient can handicap the recovery process.

TREATMENT

Nonpharmacologic Approaches
Although systematic evaluations of the effects of psychotherapy on PTSD are lacking, there is no question that such intervention occupies an important place in the management of this disorder. One goal of psychotherapy is to bring these patients to a point where their reactions are determined by the current environment, rather than by the ongoing emotional impact of earlier trauma.

Mild, acute cases of PTSD respond well to supportive psychotherapy and empathic listening, both of which can be provided by the primary care physician. That is why the physician's ability to suspect and diagnose PTSD is so important. For psychotherapy to be successful, the treating physician must become comfortable with the strong affects often exhibited by PTSD patients. Such individuals are emotionally labile, frequently highly charged with anger, but at other times pleading for tenderness, by virtue of their "victim" role.[7]

Psychotherapy can help patients deal with the guilt they may feel for having survived the trauma or for actions of commission or omission. The patient can also regain a sense of control over the environment by dealing with helpless and/or powerless feelings and the ongoing sense of vulnerability. The details of traumatic events are frequently unpleasant and evoke resistance on the part of both the patient and the therapist. Often, the meaning of the traumatic event must be explored further during therapy.

Local community support groups, such as shelters for abused women, groups for victims of incest or rape, and veterans' groups for victims of combat and/or prisoners of war, can be helpful. However, before referring patients, the physician should ensure that the group stresses a positive approach and is led by a qualified professional.

Educating the patient and the family is an essential step in treatment. It is helpful to explain the features of PTSD to the patient as well as to significant family members (see the patient information aid in the

Appendix). The physician should describe how severe trauma affects people, including the fact that the reaction could become prolonged, especially if not adequately treated, and that response to treatment may be somewhat delayed. When medication is being used to treat chronic PTSD, for example, it is important for patients to understand that improvement may take place slowly over several weeks.

The use of relaxation techniques and/or biofeedback can be helpful in providing the patient with a growing sense of control. Physical disabilities resulting from the trauma may require further attention. Self-esteem rises if the patient is able to obtain employment; vocational rehabilitation services may be beneficial in this regard. Continuing PTSD imposes stress on the patient's spouse or other immediate family members, who often require support or counseling as well. On the other hand, family members can play an important role in promoting the patient's independence and facilitating social relationships and interaction.

Pharmacologic Approaches
When the patient is severely agitated or very distressed, pharmacologic therapy has a place in the treatment of acute PTSD; it also frequently has a place in the management of chronic PTSD. The principal goals of pharmacotherapy are to induce symptom remission, distance the patient from the emotional impact and disruptive influence of the trauma, improve morale, and promote autonomic stability. Achievement of these goals will, in itself, help the patient substantially.

Although studies conducted thus far have been uncontrolled, several agents have shown promise in the treatment of PTSD. Tricyclic antidepressants, monoamine oxidase (MAO) inhibitors, and benzodiazepines have been used in both acute and chronic PTSD.[8,9] Lithium, carbamazepine, neuroleptic agents, beta blockers, and clonidine have been used in selected cases of chronic PTSD.[8,9]

A tricyclic antidepressant is often used as first-line treatment. The upper dosage limit is determined by either the patient's improvement or the development of untoward side effects. Treatment should continue for a minimum of eight weeks before the physician decides whether or not benefits have been realized. Expected improvement consists of mood elevation, improved sleep, control over affective ability, diminished nightmares, and increased social activities. The avoidance symptoms may also lessen, but such responses often take longer and may require additional psychotherapy. Secondary gain or compensation can be a limiting factor in symptom improvement.[8,10]

Should a tricyclic antidepressant prove ineffective, other medications may be tried in conjunction with referral. An MAO inhibitor might be the next step. Carbamazepine (Tegretol®) or lithium may be used if there is substance abuse or lack of impulse control. Neuroleptic agents should not be used in the routine treatment of PTSD, but are useful in patients with psychotic symptoms. Benzodiazepines may be helpful, particularly if multiple severe anxiety symptoms are also present.[8,10]

MANAGEMENT

Complications

Complicating emerging mental problems, such as drug or alcohol abuse, depression, or suicidal, homicidal, or destructive behavior, should be addressed in an appropriate way. Litigation can be a complication of PTSD arising from man-made trauma. Successful outcome of litigation does not, however, always lead to a reduction in PTSD symptoms. Other complications may include the loss of a job or the breakup of the family.

Treatment Failures

Persistence of symptoms for several months following the trauma, despite early intervention, signals the need to rethink the diagnosis (consider an affective disorder) and the treatment plan, and consider additional therapeutic strategies. If pharmacotherapy was withheld initially, it might become indicated. There may also be a need to reinvolve the patient's family and consider other social support groups. Referral to a mental health service for consultation may be helpful.

Patients with PTSD require and respond to support. The physician should meet with such patients initially as often as needed and, subsequently, every week or two.

TERMINATING THERAPY

Approximately 50 percent of PTSD victims will improve within six months of the trauma (Davidson JRT, Hughes D, Blazer DG, et al, unpublished data). Once the patient feels able to manage stress in a more controlled and/or less labile fashion, one of the principal goals of treatment has been achieved. Indications for termination of therapy include the ability to function without medication (if drug therapy had previously been necessary), the return of morale and self-esteem, the conviction that it has been possible to integrate the meaning of the trauma into present life, and restoration of social and/or occupational functioning.

REFERRAL

The primary care physician should consider referring patients with PTSD, preferably to a psychiatrist, if there are significant complicating factors, such as a high potential for violence or self-destructive behavior, substance abuse, or failure of first-line treatment. Referral to a psychiatrist may also be appropriate for patients with special pharmacologic considerations, such as physically ill individuals who are already taking medications that may interact adversely with psychotropic drugs.

References

1. Pilowsky I: Cryptotrauma and "accident neurosis." *Br J Psychiatry* 1985; 147:310-311.
2. American Psychiatric Association: *Diagnostic and Statistical Manual of Mental Disorders*, Third Edition — Revised. Washington, DC, American Psychiatric Association, 1987.
3. Helzer JE, Robins LN, McEvoy L: Posttraumatic stress disorder in the general population: Findings of the Epidemiologic Catchment Area survey. *N Engl J Med* 1987;317:1630-1634.
4. Andreasen NC: Posttraumatic stress disorder, in Kaplan HI, Freedman AM, Sadock BJ (eds): *Comprehensive Textbook of Psychiatry.* Baltimore, Williams & Wilkins, 1980, pp 1517-1525.
5. MacFarlane AC: The longitudinal course of posttraumatic morbidity. *J Nerv Ment Dis* 1988;176:30-39.
6. West LJ, Coburn K: Posttraumatic anxiety, in Pasnau R (ed): *Diagnosis and Treatment of Anxiety Disorders.* Washington, DC, APA Press, 1984, pp 79-114.
7. Kardiner A: *The Traumatic Neurosis of War.* New York, Paul Hober, 1941.
8. Davidson JRT: Biological aspects of posttraumatic stress disorder, in Prasad A J (ed): *Biological Basis and Therapy of Neuroses.* Boca Raton, Fla, CRC Press, 1988.
9. Friedman MJ: Toward rational pharmacotherapy for posttraumatic stress disorder: An interim report. *Am J Psychiatry* 1988;145:281-285.
10. van der Kolk BA: The drug treatment of posttraumatic stress disorder. *J Affective Disord* 1987;13:203-213.

CLINICAL PRESENTATION

unrelated to panic disorder

A phobia is a persistent, excessive, and unreasonable fear of a circumscribed stimulus that leads an individual to avoid the stimulus. Common simple phobias include fears of animals or insects, heights, and air travel.

Symptoms of simple phobia include anxiety-related somatic complaints, insomnia related to anticipatory anxiety, and depression related to failure to master the fear. The diagnosis of simple phobia is made only if the avoidant behavior interferes with the patient's normal routine.

TREATMENT

Nonpharmacologic Approach

Graduated in vivo exposure to the feared situation, based on the patient's fear hierarchy. (Pharmacologic treatment is usually unnecessary, except for fear of flying.)

CASE HISTORY

Joan S., a 37-year-old housewife, who had no previous history of emotional problems, was attacked by a large dog while at a local park with her two small children. The dog suddenly appeared and rushed at her, knocking her down. She suffered severe lacerations of her face, arms, and legs before the dog's owner was able to control the animal. Her primary care physician treated her in a local emergency room; her lacerations required over 100 sutures.

Following the incident, Joan became increasingly frightened of encountering dogs. Whenever she heard a dog bark, she experienced pronounced anxiety symptoms, including hyperventilation. She began to suffer from insomnia. Her husband brought her to see their primary care physician.

The primary care physician made the diagnosis of simple phobia and referred Joan to a psychiatrist who specialized in behavior therapy. After a 10-week period of systematic desensitization therapy, she was completely free of symptoms and able to resume her normal activities.

A phobia is a persistent, excessive, and unreasonable fear of a circumscribed stimulus (object, activity, or situation) that leads an individual to avoid the stimulus. Phobias are common as well as diverse.

CLINICAL PRESENTATION

A simple phobia is sometimes referred to as "specific" phobia. It is characterized by the arousal of anxiety in, and avoidance of, a specific situation or circumstance. Patients experience significant distress, which is compounded by the realization that their fears are unreasonable or excessive. Among the most common simple phobias are fears of animals such as dogs, cats, snakes, and mice; insects such as spiders; heights; lightning and/or thunder; and air travel. Agoraphobia (fear of being in a place or a situation from which escape might be difficult, or in which help might not be available in the event of a panic attack) is not a simple phobia; it is a complication of panic disorder (see Panic Disorder With or Without Agoraphobia).

As long as the situation or circumstance can be avoided, the patient is free of symptoms. If, however, the phobic situation has to be encountered, the patient first experiences anticipatory anxiety and then, on encountering the situation, becomes increasingly anxious until the situation is terminated.

In addition to the various somatic complaints associated with anxiety, the patient may experience insomnia related to anticipatory anxiety and feelings of depression related to failure to master the fear. Although simple phobias are circumscribed, the problem may lead to limited disability. For example, patients who fear air travel may not be able to meet the demands of their jobs. Phobics who avoid injections may defer needed health care. Patients who have a fear of seeing blood may faint on encountering the feared situation. Here, as anxiety mounts, the heart rate slows and blood pressure drops — an example of a vasovagal response to fear.

Patients with simple phobias are generally aware of the unreasonable nature of their fears. Nevertheless, despite reassurance, their fears persist. When interference with normal functioning results, an individual may seek assistance.

Phobias may occur as part of more complex anxiety disorders. Before diagnosing simple phobia, it is critically important to be certain that the patient has never had any unexpected or unprovoked attacks of anxiety (i.e., panic attacks), which signal the presence of panic disorder.

EPIDEMIOLOGY

The simple phobias are among the most common of mental disorders. The Epidemiologic Catchment Area survey found that the lifetime prevalence rates of simple phobia were approximately 4 percent for men and 9 percent for women.[1] Many people with simple phobias, however, do not seek care.

ETIOLOGY

It appears that humans are biologically prepared to learn fear connections rapidly with certain stimuli. These stimuli form the range of common fears, the function of which appears to be to confer protection on young children as they explore the environment. Thus, fears of heights, snakes and other small animals, loud noises, and so on would function to protect children from exploring potentially dangerous situations. Although most common fears dissipate with age, as would be expected with a protective mechanism, some appear to develop into phobias. Such development may occur because of an unfortunate experience with a particular situation, e.g., being frightened by a large dog. More often, common fears may be enhanced by fearful communication within the family. Evidence from primate studies, for example, shows that young monkeys learn fears faster when their parents show fear than when a strange primate exhibits the same fear.[2] Whether or not genetic transmission of specific phobias occurs is not yet clear.

Phobias often have deep roots that are based on errors in the original learning situation. Simple phobias often develop out of specific upsetting events. While some of these phobias may fade with time, others persist indefinitely. Maladaptive behaviors used as coping mechanisms may in fact exacerbate the situation.

TREATMENT

The most effective form of treatment for the majority of the simple phobias is graduated exposure to the feared situation. With the exception of fear of flying (see below), pharmacologic treatment is usually unnecessary.

The foundation for successful treatment is an accurate history in which the hierarchical arrangement of feared situations is clearly explicated. For example, a height phobia may increase not only with increasing height, but also according to the perception of the safety of the situation. Thus, looking through a closed window 50 feet above the ground may be less anxiety provoking than looking down from an open balcony 30 feet above the ground. Once the fear hierarchy is established, instructions to practice entering the feared situation should be given, beginning with the least fear-provoking situation. Once that situation fails to provoke fear, exposure to the next fearful situation in the hierarchy may begin, and so on. This process desensitizes the specific phobia. Patients can often carry out the exposure program by themselves, with occasional supervision by the therapist.

The exposure program must consist of "real life" exposure to the feared object or situation. Exposure lasting longer than one and one-half hours is more successful than that lasting less than one hour. Prolonged exposure allows the patient to develop natural relaxation. Short exposure tends to provide premature release from the phobic stimulus.

To facilitate supervision by the therapist, and to allow the patient to perceive progress better, the patient should be asked to keep a record. The record should include the situation, the anxiety experienced in it, and the date of each exposure practice. This allows the therapist to praise the patient for progress, and to uncover quickly any problems in the exposure regimen. Such problems usually occur when the patient attempts too big a step, often resulting in a setback. If this happens, the hierarchy of feared situations should be reconstructed to allow for smaller steps in the exposure program. Sometimes a failure to advance is due to the patient's exaggerated perception of the dangers involved in the phobic situation. In such cases it will be necessary to explore these thoughts and to help the patient correct them using education about the reality of such cognitions. Most phobias resolve with a few hours of practice.

Fear of Flying

Fear of air travel is one of the most common simple phobias for which patients seek treatment. Unfortunately, it is particularly difficult to arrange for graduated practice since the patient cannot leave the feared situation once the airplane takes off. One approach is to refer such patients to a "Fear of Flying Clinic," many of which are sponsored by airlines. In such programs, education and exposure are combined in a group setting, ending with a practice flight or two.

An alternative, more palliative, approach is the use of medication during flights. A benzodiazepine, taken two hours before the flight and repeated at indicated intervals if necessary until the patient reaches the destination, diminishes the symptoms of anxiety and also reduces fearful cognitions, resulting in a comfortable flight. The dose of medication may need to be altered after the first flight, either increasing or, less frequently, decreasing the dose. Excellent results can be expected from this simple treatment, and occasionally, after repeated exposure, the patient will recover from the fear of flying (i.e., be able to make trips without resorting to the use of medication). *Patients should be cautioned not to use alcohol in conjunction with the medication because of the risks of sedation and amnesia.*

MANAGEMENT

Although simple phobia is a chronic condition, graduated exposure usually results in partial or complete remission of symptoms. Relapse may occur, however, in which case a further course of exposure treatment is indicated. No complications of treatment are usually expected. Treatment failure is usually the result of either difficulty in arranging for exposure to the phobic situation, or the complexity or unusual nature of the phobia. In such cases, the primary care physician should consider referral.

REFERRAL

Many simple phobias can be treated with exposure instructions given by the primary care physician. However, in cases of complex or intense simple phobia, or treatment failure, referral may be indicated. Since medication is not usually indicated in the treatment of simple phobias, referral may be either to a psychiatrist or a psychologist. In either case it is important to select a therapist experienced in exposure therapy. Anxiety disorder clinics are located in many major medical centers, and are an excellent source of treatment for phobias. Referral centers also can be found in many metropolitan areas.

References

1. Robins LN, Helzer JE, Weissman MM, et al: Lifetime prevalence of specific psychiatric disorders in three sites. *Arch Gen Psychiatry* 1984;41:949-958.
2. Mineka S: Animal models of anxiety-based disorders: Their usefulness and limitations. In Tuma AH, Maser J (eds): *Anxiety and the Anxiety Disorders*. Erlbaum, Hillsdale, NJ, pp 199-244.

CLINICAL PRESENTATION

Social phobia is a common disorder characterized by episodes of intense anxiety related to actual or anticipated social situations involving possible scrutiny by others. Presentations of social phobia seen frequently in primary care practice are performance anxiety, such as excessive fear of speaking in front of a group, and avoidance of routine activities, such as eating or writing while observed, because of concerns about behaving in a way that might be humiliating or embarrassing.

Although social phobia is a distinct diagnosis, some of its symptoms occur in other disorders.

Symptoms on exposure to the phobic stimulus include blushing, tachycardia and palpitations, tremulousness, perspiration, and dyspnea.

TREATMENT

Nonpharmacologic Approaches

- Behavior therapy techniques such as exposure, social skills training, systematic desensitization, "flooding," anxiety management training, and relaxation training
- Cognitive restructuring

Pharmacologic Approaches

Medications from the following classes have been found effective in treating some cases of social phobia:

- Beta blockers
- MAO inhibitors
- Benzodiazepines

CASE HISTORY

Paul W., a 42-year-old electrical engineer, presented to his primary care physician complaining of performance anxiety that was interfering with his work. Whenever he had to give an oral presentation (a necessity that was becoming increasingly more frequent), he experienced a pounding heart and sweaty palms, and felt intensely uneasy. Because he dreaded speaking before groups, his presentations were poor, and his professional advancement was threatened.

Paul's physician diagnosed social phobia and prescribed propranolol, 20 mg, to be taken 45 minutes to an hour before giving a speech. On a follow-up visit several months later, Paul reported that his symptoms had improved markedly. He needed to use the medication only on rare occasions, before presentations to very large audiences. Although Paul stated that he would "never be the life of the party," he now felt more comfortable being the subject of others' attention, and he felt that his career prospects had improved.

The experience of increased anxiety in certain social or performance situations, such as during public speaking or a job interview, is common and typically benign. For most people, social anxiety never becomes excessive or debilitating and may even serve a useful function. In an individual with social phobia, however, anxiety is excessive and unreasonable, often impairs social and occupational functioning, and is the source of marked distress. Although social phobia is relatively common, it has only recently become the object of scientific study.

CLINICAL PRESENTATION

The essential feature of social phobia is a persistent fear and avoidance of one or more situations in which the person is exposed to possible scrutiny by others and fears that he or she may do something or act in a way that will be humiliating or embarrassing.[1] Patients may have a fear of being unable to talk when speaking in front of a group, of being watched when eating, of being unable to urinate when using a public restroom, or of experiencing uncontrollable trembling of the hands when attempting to write while being observed.

Often, individuals with social phobia both fear and avoid a variety of social situations.[2] Episodes of anxiety and autonomic discharge may occur in one or more circumstances. The symptom pattern typically includes blushing, tachycardia and palpitations, tremulousness, perspiration, and dyspnea in anticipation of, and during, phobic encounters.

The extent of phobic avoidance varies considerably among individuals. Many people are successful in their occupations and manage to avoid phobic activities, but may do so at the expense of career advancement and self-esteem. Others report that they do not actually avoid certain activities, but suffer intense anticipatory and situational anxiety, as well as dread. Often, a cycle is established in which anticipatory anxiety results in impaired performance, in turn leading to phobic avoidance and the maintenance of fear. Many patients with social phobia also suffer from depression.

The answers to several important questions concerning the patient's experience of anxiety symptoms, phobic avoidance, and thoughts about social interaction will help in identifying social phobia.

The clinician should ask the individual to describe the psychological and somatic symptoms that occur in association with anxiety. What situations elicit these symptoms? Is the experience of anxiety predictable (situationally cued), or is its onset unpredictable and spontaneous, as in panic disorder? What situations are avoided? What is the patient's primary reason for avoiding these situations?

Individuals with social phobia typically report that their anxiety is primarily situational. They are preoccupied with fears of negative evaluation and embarrassment, rather than fears of going crazy, losing control, and dying, which are typically associated with panic disorder. Furthermore, patients with social phobia are poor judges of their own social behavior. They tend to underestimate their social competence, while overestimating the degree to which their anxiety is perceived by others. They are often acutely aware of somatic signs of anxiety (such as blushing, sweating, and trembling) and believe these symptoms are obvious to others.

Social phobia may occur as a complication of panic disorder, in which case panic disorder is considered the primary disorder and the social phobia should be treated in the same manner as any phobia occurring as a complication of panic disorder. It is therefore important to consider any history of unprovoked or unexpected attacks that include the characteristic symptom cluster (see Panic Disorder With or Without Agoraphobia). Social avoidance and interpersonal anxiety are associated with other mental illnesses as well, including depressive, schizophrenic, and personality disorders.

EPIDEMIOLOGY

Preliminary findings from the Epidemiologic Catchment Area survey have shown that the six-month prevalence rate of social phobia in two urban samples ranged from 1.5 to 2.6 percent for women and from 0.9 to 1.7 percent for men.[3] Social phobia showed a more equal sex distribution than did agoraphobia and panic disorder, which showed a marked female predominance. Without treatment, social phobia seems to follow a fairly chronic and unremitting course.

ETIOLOGY

Both biological and psychological hypotheses have been advanced to explain the etiology of social phobia. Among its hypothesized causes are neuroendocrine or neurotransmitter-receptor abnormalities, genetic factors, traumatic or negative learning experiences, social skill deficits, and faulty cognitive appraisal patterns. It is unclear which of these variables makes the largest contribution to the development of this syndrome.

TREATMENT

Despite the prevalence and potential seriousness of social phobia, no single therapy is recommended for this disorder. Both behavior and pharmacologic therapies have been found to be effective[4]; however, behavior therapy is the treatment of first choice.

Nonpharmacologic Approaches
Several clinical studies have suggested that cognitive and behavior therapies may be effective in treating performance anxiety and other forms of social phobia.[4-8] Varying degrees of success have been achieved with techniques such as exposure, social skills training, systematic desensitization, "flooding," anxiety management training, relaxation training, and cognitive restructuring (see Nonpharmacologic Treatment in Part One). Behavior therapists base their interventions on the assumption that patients with social phobia have learned maladaptive anxiety responses to social situations and that these responses can be unlearned or replaced with more adaptive coping behaviors or skills.

Behavior therapy is typically provided in a group setting, so that patients have the opportunity to confront the phobic situation while learning and rehearsing new skills. Such therapy may be employed as an alternative or an adjunct to pharmacotherapy. Although cognitive-behavior techniques are not yet standard therapy in primary care, several recent studies have demonstrated some success with them.

Pharmacologic Approaches
Evidence suggests that social phobia is responsive to pharmacologic therapy. To date, most research on the outcomes of such treatment has examined responses to three types of drugs—beta blockers, monoamine oxidase (MAO) inhibitors, and benzodiazepines.

Beta blockers. Patients with circumscribed social fears who experience symptoms in only a limited number of predictable situations (and who do not have significant generalized anxiety or depressed mood) may benefit from medication administered on an as-needed basis (just prior to confronting the specific social situations that provoke anxiety). Beta blockers such as propranolol (Inderal®), 10 to 40 mg taken 45 to 60 minutes before the feared activity, have been used successfully in individuals with performance anxiety.[9] These agents reduce somatic responses to phobic situations and should facilitate performance by modifying the physical experience of anxiety. "Stage fright" and "examination nerves" (i.e., excessive anxiety associated with academic tests) are two types of performance anxiety that have been treated successfully with beta blockers.

Patients with more generalized social fears may respond better to medication administered on a daily basis. The cardioselective beta blocker atenolol (Tenormin®), 50 to 100 mg/day, has been used with some success in patients with more generalized forms of social phobia.[9]

In patients who can take beta blockers safely, these agents may provide good initial treatment of social phobia, because the side effects are typically limited to fatigue.

The usual contraindications to the use of beta blockers, which include a history of bronchial asthma, congestive heart failure, or significant bradycardia, should be observed.

MAO inhibitors. Studies have indicated that the MAO inhibitor phenelzine (Nardil®), up to 90 mg/day, reduces situationally cued anxiety and may be helpful in increasing social interaction.[5,10] Several weeks of treatment are required to achieve therapeutic efficacy; the minimum length of an adequate phenelzine trial is considered to be four weeks. One drawback to treatment with this agent is the requirement that patients adhere to a diet low in tyramine to protect against hypertensive crises. Individuals unlikely to comply with the drug regimen or dietary restrictions should not be considered for phenelzine therapy.

Benzodiazepines. Preliminary indications from case reports and ongoing clinical trials suggest that alprazolam (Xanax®) may be beneficial in some pa-

tients.[5,11,12] There are no known well-controlled clinical trials of other benzodiazepines in the treatment of social phobia. Alprazolam can either be taken on an as-needed basis (shortly before the patient confronts a phobic situation) or daily, in divided doses, if symptoms are severe and disabling. The initial therapeutic effects of alprazolam are usually evident immediately or within a few weeks of treatment initiation.

MANAGEMENT

Many patients discover that alcohol, anxiolytics, or other self-administered drugs provide temporary relief of anxiety symptoms. The primary care physician therefore needs to be alert to the possibility of substance use or abuse and prepared to intervene if necessary.

Long-term studies are not yet available to determine the optimum length of pharmacologic treatment when indicated for prevention of relapse. Based on experience in treating other forms of anxiety, continuous therapy of six to 12 months is probably required after remission is attained.

Supportive counseling throughout the course of therapy, including such simple measures as urging the patient to restrict use of alcohol, advising regular use of the prescribed medication for as long as indicated, and encouraging frequent and prolonged contact with the phobic stimulus, is recommended.

Since no single medication is preferred for the treatment of social phobia, the physician may wish to give one agent a thorough trial, then switch to a second class of drugs, or even a third, if necessary, until therapeutic benefit has been achieved.

References

1. American Psychiatric Association: *Diagnostic and Statistical Manual of Mental Disorders*, Third Edition — Revised. Washington, DC, American Psychiatric Association, 1987, p 243.
2. Amies PL, Gelder MG, Shaw PM: Social phobia: A comparative clinical study. *Br J Psychiatry* 1983;142:174-179.
3. Myers JK, Weissman MM, Tischler GL, et al: Six-month prevalence of psychiatric disorders in three communities: 1980-1982. *Arch Gen Psychiatry* 1984; 41:959-967.
4. Arnkoff DB, Glass CR, Shea CA, et al: Client predispositions toward cognitive and social skills treatments for shyness. *J Integrative Eclectic Psychother* 1987;6: 154-164.

5. Shea CA, Uhde TW, Cimbolic P, et al: Social phobia: Behavioral versus drug therapies. In Uhde TW, Shea CA (eds): *Social Phobia: Understanding and Treatment.* Symposium presented at the annual meeting of the American Psychiatric Association, Montreal, Canada, May 1988.

6. Glass CR, Shea CA: Cognitive therapy for shyness and social anxiety. In Jones WH, Cheek JM, Briggs SR (eds): *Shyness: Perspectives on Research and Treatment.* New York, Plenum, pp 315-327.

7. Heimberg RG, Dodge CS, Becker RE: Social phobia. In Michelson L, Ascher LM (eds): *Anxiety and Stress Disorders: Cognitive-Behavioral Assessment and Treatment.* New York, Guilford, 1987, pp 280-309.

8. Matlick RP, Peters L: Treatment of severe social phobia: Effects of guided exposure with and without cognitive restructuring. *J Consult Clin Psychol* 56:251-260.

9. Gorman JM, Gorman LK: Drug treatment of social phobia. *J Affective Disord* 1987; 13:183-192.

10. Levin AP, Liebowitz MR: Drug treatment of phobias: Efficacy and optimum use. *Drugs* 1987;34:504-514.

11. Lydiard RB, Laraia MT, Howell EF, et al: Alprazolam in the treatment of social phobia. *J Clin Psychiatry* 1988;49:17-19.

12. Reich J, Yates W: A pilot study of treatment of social phobia with alprazolam. *Am J Psychiatry* 1988;145:590-594.

Appendices

A variety of psychiatric rating scales and structured interviews have been developed for evaluating patients with mental disorders. The interview schedules are primarily diagnostic, while the rating scales are better at measuring severity and changes over time and can help target areas needing improvement. Assessment tools can provide useful guidelines for the primary care physician, especially when more precise information will help clarify the nature of the patient's illness and permit more effective therapy.

This section provides examples of three assessment tools that may be of assistance to the primary care physician: the Sheehan Patient Rated Anxiety Scale, the Beck Depression Inventory, and the CAGE Questionnaire for Alcoholism.

Features

- Patient-administered
- Identifies and measures severity of symptoms associated with anxiety

Scoring and interpretation: Assign a value of 0 to the first answer column ("Not At All"), 1 to the second column, 2 to the third, and so on. Scores above 30 are usually considered abnormal, and scores above 80 are severe. The mean score in panic disorder and agoraphobia is 57 ± 20. The goal of treatment is to bring the score below 20.

SHEEHAN PATIENT RATED ANXIETY SCALE

During the past week, how much did you suffer from...
(Check only one answer for each question.)

0. Not At All   1. A Little   2. Moderately   3. Quite A Bit   4. Extremely

		0	1	2	3	4
1.	Difficulty in getting your breath, smothering, or overbreathing.	☐	☐	☐	☐	☐
2.	Choking sensation or lump in throat.	☐	☐	☐	☐	☐
3.	Skipping, racing, or pounding of your heart.	☐	☐	☐	☐	☐
4.	Chest pain, pressure, or discomfort.	☐	☐	☐	☐	☐
5.	Bouts of excessive sweating.	☐	☐	☐	☐	☐
6.	Faintness, light-headedness, or dizzy spells.	☐	☐	☐	☐	☐
7.	Sensation of rubbery or "jelly" legs.	☐	☐	☐	☐	☐
8.	Feeling off balance or unsteady like you might fall.	☐	☐	☐	☐	☐
9.	Nausea or stomach problems.	☐	☐	☐	☐	☐
10.	Feeling that things around you are strange, unreal, foggy, or detached from you.	☐	☐	☐	☐	☐
11.	Feeling outside or detached from part or all of your body, or a floating feeling.	☐	☐	☐	☐	☐
12.	Tingling or numbness in parts of your body.	☐	☐	☐	☐	☐
13.	Hot flashes or cold chills.	☐	☐	☐	☐	☐
14.	Shaking or trembling.	☐	☐	☐	☐	☐
15.	Having a fear that you are dying or that something terrible is about to happen.	☐	☐	☐	☐	☐
16.	Feeling you are losing control or going insane.	☐	☐	☐	☐	☐
17.	Sudden anxiety attacks with three or more of the symptoms (listed above) that occur when you are in or about to go into a situation that is likely, from your experience, to bring on an attack.	☐	☐	☐	☐	☐

SHEEHAN PATIENT RATED ANXIETY SCALE (Continued)

0. Not At All   1. A Little   2. Moderately   3. Quite A Bit   4. Extremely

	0	1	2	3	4
18. Sudden unexpected anxiety attacks with three or more symptoms (listed above) that occur with little or no provocation (i.e., when you are **NOT** in a situation that is likely, from your experience, to bring on an attack).	☐	☐	☐	☐	☐
19. Sudden unexpected spells with only one or two symptoms (listed above) that occur with little or no provocation (i.e., when you are **NOT** in a situation that is likely, from your experience, to bring on an attack).	☐	☐	☐	☐	☐
20. Anxiety episodes that build up as you anticipate doing something that is likely, from your experience, to bring on anxiety that is more intense than most people experience in such situations.	☐	☐	☐	☐	☐
21. Avoiding situations because they frighten you.	☐	☐	☐	☐	☐
22. Being dependent on others.	☐	☐	☐	☐	☐
23. Tension and inability to relax.	☐	☐	☐	☐	☐
24. Anxiety, nervousness, restlessness.	☐	☐	☐	☐	☐
25. Spells of increased sensitivity to sound, light, or touch.	☐	☐	☐	☐	☐
26. Attacks of diarrhea.	☐	☐	☐	☐	☐
27. Worrying about your health too much.	☐	☐	☐	☐	☐
28. Feeling tired, weak, and exhausted easily.	☐	☐	☐	☐	☐
29. Headaches or pains in neck or head.	☐	☐	☐	☐	☐
30. Difficulty in falling asleep.	☐	☐	☐	☐	☐
31. Waking in the middle of the night, or restless sleep.	☐	☐	☐	☐	☐
32. Unexpected waves of depression occurring with little or no provocation.	☐	☐	☐	☐	☐
33. Emotions and moods going up and down a lot in response to changes around you.	☐	☐	☐	☐	☐
34. Recurrent and persistent ideas, thoughts, impulses, or images that are intrusive, unwanted, senseless, or repugnant.	☐	☐	☐	☐	☐
35. Having to repeat the same action in a ritual, e.g., checking, washing, counting repeatedly, when it's not really necessary.	☐	☐	☐	☐	☐

Reprinted with permission from Sheehan DV.

Features

- Patient-administered
- Identifies and measures severity of symptoms associated with depression
- Uses *DSM-III* depressive criteria

Note: May not differentiate between moderate and severe depression

Scoring and interpretation: Assign a value of 0 to the first answer choice, 1 to the second, 2 to the third, and 3 to the fourth. Scores above 19 are considered to reflect clinical depression; scores above 24 indicate the need for treatment—possibly with an antidepressant medication. The goal of treatment is to bring the score below 10.

Below are samples of two of the 21 statements contained in the Beck Depression Inventory. For information on ordering the complete version, contact the publisher, The Psychological Corporation, Order Service Center, P.O. Box 9954, San Antonio, TX 78204-0954, telephone: 1-800-233-5682.

BECK DEPRESSION INVENTORY

On this questionnaire are groups of statements. Please read each group of statements carefully. Then pick out the one statement in each group that best describes the way you have been feeling the PAST WEEK, INCLUDING TODAY. Check the box beside the statement you picked. If several statements in the group seem to apply equally well, check the box for each one. *Be sure to read all the statements in each group before making your choice.*

☐ I am not particularly discouraged about the future.	☐ I can work about as well as before.
☐ I feel discouraged about the future.	☐ It takes an extra effort to get started at doing something.
☐ I feel I have nothing to look forward to.	☐ I have to push myself very hard to do anything.
☐ I feel that the future is hopeless and that things cannot improve.	☐ I can't do any work at all.

Use: Office screening for alcohol abuse for all adults who are not teetotalers

Features

- Simple, quick (less than 2 minutes)
- Very sensitive
- Can be incorporated into the medical interview or used as a previsit screening device

Scoring and Interpretation: One positive response suggests the likelihood of the presence of alcoholism and requires further exploration. Two or three affirmative answers should create a high index of suspicion. Four positive responses may be diagnostic of alcoholism.

CAGE QUESTIONNAIRE FOR ALCOHOLISM

1. Have you ever tried to **C**ut down on your drinking?
2. Are you **A**nnoyed when people ask you about your drinking?
3. Do you ever feel **G**uilty about your drinking?
4. Do you ever take a morning **E**ye-opener?

Adapted with permission from Ewing JA: Detecting alcoholism. The CAGE Questionnaire. *JAMA* 1984;252:1905-1907. Copyright © 1984 by American Medical Association.

Patient education is an important part of any treatment program. It can enhance patient cooperation, provide reassurance, and improve outcome.

This section contains information for the patient on the various anxiety and depressive disorders, and the medications used to treat them. These patient information aids may be reproduced and distributed to your patients.

ADJUSTMENT DISORDER/GENERALIZED ANXIETY DISORDER

Anxiety is an inevitable part of life. Nearly everyone experiences it at one time or another. Anxiety generally occurs as an occasional, temporary reaction to the stresses of everyday life. When anxiety becomes so severe or frequent that it interferes with a person's ability to function, an anxiety disorder may be present.

What is an anxiety disorder?

An anxiety disorder is a distinct illness with a specific set of symptoms. Two common anxiety disorders are adjustment disorder with anxiety and generalized anxiety disorder. In adjustment disorder, excessive anxiety or other emotional reactions occur in association with a difficulty in adjusting to a specific stressful situation. In generalized anxiety disorder, the excessive anxiety persists and is focused on a variety of life situations. The excessive worry, apprehension, and fear that people with anxiety disorders feel may be accompanied by physical symptoms, such as fluttery stomach, shortness of breath, and increased heart rate. Some people with anxiety disorders also experience depression.

Can anxiety disorders be treated?

Yes. Anxiety disorders can be treated effectively with counseling, medication, or both. Supportive psychotherapy can help a person explore and gradually deal with the psychological factors that may be contributing to the anxiety disorder symptoms. Relaxation, biofeedback, and meditation sometimes lessen anxiety symptoms. Several medications are available that can help some patients recover by relieving debilitating symptoms, such as excessive restlessness, muscle tension, and inability to fall asleep. These medications are safe and effective when taken as directed by your doctor. Alcohol, caffeine, and nicotine can make anxiety worse, and should be avoided. Also, check with your doctor before drinking alcoholic beverages or taking any other medication while you are on medication for your anxiety disorder.

Not all treatments and techniques work equally well for all patients. You and your doctor should decide together which combination of treatments is best for you.

Suggested Reading

Benson H: *The Relaxation Response*. New York, William Morrow, 1975.
Sheehan DV: *The Anxiety Disease*. New York, Bantam Books, 1983.

DEPRESSIVE DISORDERS

Occasional feelings of sadness are a normal part of life. When people experience sad feelings that are intense or persist for long periods of time, they are considered to be "depressed." Depressed feelings are often caused by a life crisis, such as the death of a loved one, breakup of a marriage, loss of a job, or a move away from close friends, but they also may occur for no apparent reason. When depression interferes with a person's ability to function normally, a depressive disorder may be present.

What is a depressive disorder?
A depressive disorder is an illness that affects a person's outlook on life and ability to function. People with depressive disorders feel sad, tired, and irritable. They are no longer interested in the things they once enjoyed. A depressive disorder can get worse. It can last up to several years if it is not treated. It may recur several times during a person's life and can even lead to suicide.

Can depressive disorders be treated?
Yes. Depressive disorders can be treated effectively with medication and psychotherapy, or counseling. Medication is useful in treating the biological component of a depressive disorder. Psychotherapy helps patients understand and cope with aspects of their lives that may contribute to their disorder. Since every patient is different, the best treatment for one may not be best for another. You and your doctor should decide together which treatment plan is best for you.

OBSESSIVE-COMPULSIVE DISORDER

What is obsessive-compulsive disorder?

Obsessive-compulsive disorder is an illness characterized by involuntary obsessions and compulsions that interfere with normal life. Obsessions are unwanted ideas, worries, thoughts, images, or impulses that occur repeatedly. Compulsions are behaviors that are repeated in a stereotypic manner. Obsessions often cause anxiety, and the compulsive behaviors, or rituals, serve to reduce this anxiety.

Obsessive-compulsive disorder can significantly disrupt a person's life. Obsessive thoughts or compulsive behaviors can become so time consuming and disturbing that it becomes difficult for the person to lead a normal life. The person's family life, social life, and work performance can suffer.

Unfortunately, most people with obsessive-compulsive disorder do not seek help for their illness, because they are embarrassed or ashamed, or fear that they will be judged as "crazy." Thus, many people suffer needlessly.

Can obsessive-compulsive disorder be treated?

Yes. Many people have been treated with a combination of behavior therapy and medication. Behavior therapy consists of confronting the feared situation until the anxiety lessens and delaying the compulsive behavior for longer and longer periods of time. This technique often helps reduce the symptoms and establish more normal behavior. In some cases, people with obsessive-compulsive disorder "forget" how to do certain things normally. Having someone demonstrate normal behavior is often effective in changing behavior.

Your doctor may prescribe medication if you are experiencing intense anxiety. This medication is prescribed only for short periods of time to help ease your anxiety while you are overcoming your rituals.

PANIC DISORDER

What is panic disorder?

Panic disorder is a real illness with both a physical and a psychological component. While the symptoms of panic disorder may be aggravated by stressful situations or psychological conflicts, the primary cause appears to be a biological imbalance affecting the central nervous system. Vulnerability to this biological imbalance may be inherited.

Who gets it?

Panic disorder is common. At any given time, several million Americans may be affected by it. It usually begins during the late teens or early 20s, and it can occur in both men and women. However, most people with panic disorder (about 75%) are women, probably because of some chemical or biological factors that are not yet fully understood.

What are panic attacks?

Panic attacks are sudden "spells" of intense anxiety. Typically, especially in the beginning, the attacks occur *unexpectedly*—with no warning and for no apparent reason. They may be accompanied by a variety of symptoms, including these:

- Dizziness or faintness
- Difficulty breathing
- Choking or smothering sensations
- Unsteadiness or shakiness
- Rapid, pounding, or "skipping" heartbeat
- Chest pain or pressure
- Tingling or numbness
- Nausea or diarrhea
- Feelings of "strangeness" or "unreality"
- Fear of dying, "going crazy," or losing control

Panic attacks usually last somewhere between one minute and an hour, and they occur, on average, two to four times per week. In some cases, the attacks disappear for long periods of time and then return—as before—for no apparent reason. The intensity of the attacks may fluctuate considerably, even in the same person.

Can panic attacks lead to something more serious?

Panic attacks can cause suffering and can significantly disrupt people's lives, but they are not dangerous or life-threatening. Over time, many people who experience recurrent panic attacks become increasingly anxious, even between attacks. They may develop one or more phobias, and begin to fear and avoid the places and situations where attacks have occurred—for example, crowds, elevators, highways, or bridges. They may eventually be afraid to make plans, to travel, even to shop. Their social lives, family lives, and jobs may be adversely affected.

Can panic disorder be treated?

Yes. In virtually every case, panic disorder *can* be treated successfully, usually with medication and counseling. Since every patient is different, the best treatment for one may not be best for another. You and your doctor should decide together which treatment plan is best for you.

Suggested Reading
Marks IM: *Living With Fear*. New York, McGraw-Hill, 1978.
Sheehan DV: *The Anxiety Disease*. New York, Bantam Books, 1986.
Weekes C: *Peace From Nervous Suffering*. New York, Bantam Books, 1978.

POSTTRAUMATIC STRESS DISORDER

What is posttraumatic stress disorder?

Posttraumatic stress disorder is a severe reaction to a traumatic event that is outside the range of usual human experience and that would be distressing to almost anyone—such as a serious accident, natural disaster, assault, rape, or military combat.

Can posttraumatic stress disorder be treated?

Yes. Several psychological and behavioral therapies are effective in treating this disorder, and various medications are available to relieve debilitating symptoms.

Psychotherapy can help people with posttraumatic stress disorder put the earlier trauma behind them and deal more effectively with the current situation where the trauma does not exist. Supportive counseling or group psychotherapy for people suffering from similar experiences (e.g., combat, rape) may also be helpful.

Because the symptoms of this disorder can be disabling, your physician may prescribe certain medications to ease the disturbed sleep, anxiety, and depression that are common. Once these disruptive symptoms are controlled, you will begin to feel better, stronger, and more able to cope with and overcome the trauma. Medication may be required for a period of weeks to months.

Family counseling, relaxation therapy, and biofeedback may be helpful to you while other treatments are in progress. Ask your doctor to discuss these therapies with you.

SIMPLE PHOBIA

What is simple phobia?

A simple phobia is an excessive fear of an object, activity, or a situation, which leads a person to avoid the cause of that fear. Some of the more common simple phobias are fears of animals (such as dogs, cats, snakes, and mice), insects (such as spiders), heights, enclosed spaces, and flying.

A simple phobia can seriously disrupt a person's social and vocational life. For example, a fear of flying can restrict a person from traveling for business or pleasure. A fear of animals can keep a person from visiting close friends because of a family pet. If the phobia is not treated, it can become worse and the person's life can become more restricted.

Can simple phobia be treated?

Yes. Simple phobia can be treated effectively with a technique known as exposure therapy. It involves graduated exposure to the feared object or situation. By working with your physician or a therapist, you can discover the cause of your fear, learn to face it, and gradually overcome it. Many patients have successfully overcome their fears with such treatment. Ask your doctor to discuss exposure therapy with you. For fear of flying, your doctor may prescribe medication temporarily until the fear has subsided.

SOCIAL PHOBIA

What is social phobia?

Social phobia is a fear of certain social situations because they may prove either embarrassing or humiliating. It is a very common disorder. Examples of social phobias are fears of public speaking, using public restrooms, eating or writing in public, engaging in conversation with others, and using public transportation. Because people with social phobia try to avoid the social situations that they fear, their personal lives and job performance are often affected.

Can social phobia be treated?

Yes. Social phobia can be treated with medication and/or behavior therapy. When a person's major symptom is a rapid heart rate, a medication called a beta blocker, which is used to treat hypertension, may be prescribed. Beta blockers are especially effective for fear of public speaking or performing. Your doctor will determine whether you need medication and when or how often it should be taken.

Behavior therapy involves repeated exposure to the feared situation, which ultimately helps reduce anxiety and fear. A type of psychotherapy called cognitive therapy helps people understand the irrational basis of their fears and adopt a more rational approach to deal with them. Group therapy helps some people confront and overcome their fears by practicing new skills in a social setting. You and your doctor can decide together which combination of treatments is best for you.

Suggested Reading
Marks IM: *Living With Fear.* New York, McGraw-Hill, 1978.

WHAT YOU SHOULD KNOW ABOUT BENZODIAZEPINES

When taken as prescribed by a physician, benzodiazepines are safe, effective medication used to treat certain anxiety disorders.

Beneficial Effects

Benzodiazepines have been found to greatly reduce anxiety in many patients. You will probably begin to feel better within a few days to a few weeks. It is important that you follow your doctor's instructions exactly concerning how much and when to take the medication. Do *not* take any more or less than the prescribed dose, and do *not* take the medication more or less often than your doctor has directed. Your doctor may intend to gradually (and safely) increase the dosage in order to find the best dosage for you. If you have been taking this medication regularly, do not stop taking it without checking with your doctor.

Precautions

- If you are pregnant, intend to become pregnant, or are breast-feeding, inform your doctor before taking this medication.

- This medication can add to the effects of alcohol or other central nervous system depressants (drugs that slow down the nervous system), possibly causing serious adverse reactions, including severe drowsiness, amnesia, and unconsciousness. Check with your doctor before drinking alcoholic beverages or taking any other drugs while you are on this medication.

- Know how you react to this medication before operating any machinery or driving a car. Benzodiazepines can cause drowsiness.

- Tell your doctor if you are allergic to or are taking *any* medications, either prescription or non-prescription.

Possible Side Effects

Some patients may experience mild side effects, such as blurred vision, clumsiness, unsteadiness, light-headedness, drowsiness, headache, or unusual tiredness or weakness while taking this medication. Such effects generally occur at the beginning of therapy and usually disappear within a few weeks. They are not dangerous, but if they are bothersome, tell your doctor. Your dosage can be adjusted to minimize them.

If you experience severe side effects, such as shortness of breath, skin rash or itching, muscle weakness, seizures, or any other unusual symptoms, tell your doctor immediately.

WHAT YOU SHOULD KNOW ABOUT BETA BLOCKERS FOR PERFORMANCE ANXIETY

Beta blockers are safe, effective medications that are often prescribed for high blood pressure or chest pain, but are also used to treat the symptoms associated with the fear of public speaking or performing, commonly known as "stage fright." Beta blockers reduce the rapid heart rate, flushing, and sweating people often feel when they are about to go on stage or face a group of people. Because such symptoms occur only when a person is about to perform, the medication is taken shortly before — usually one-half hour or so before — the event.

Precautions

- If you are pregnant, intend to become pregnant, or are breast-feeding, inform your doctor before taking this medication.

- Tell your doctor if you are taking any medication to control high blood pressure, asthma, or heart or lung disease.

- Let your doctor know if you are allergic to any medication, either prescription or nonprescription.

- Because beta blockers can cause dizziness, drowsiness, light-headedness, or make you feel less alert than usual, you should determine how you react to this medication before you drive a car or operate a machine.

- If you have been taking this medication regularly, do not stop taking it suddenly. Taper it according to your doctor's instructions.

Possible Side Effects

Because people with performance anxiety usually take this medication only in small doses and for a short time, side effects are not usually a problem. However, if you notice any unusual or troublesome symptoms, inform your doctor.

WHAT YOU SHOULD KNOW ABOUT MAO INHIBITORS

MAO inhibitors are used to treat depression, certain anxiety disorders, and other illnesses.

Precautions

Before taking this medication, tell your doctor if you are allergic to any medicine, either prescription or nonprescription, and if you are pregnant, intend to become pregnant while using this medication, or are breast-feeding.

Certain foods, beverages, and drugs must be avoided while you are taking an MAO inhibitor (see Table 1). In general, it is best to check with your doctor before taking *any* prescription or nonprescription drug during the time you are taking an MAO inhibitor. And make sure that *all* your doctors and dentists know about *all* the drugs you are taking.

Possible Side Effects

Many patients experience no side effects at all while taking MAO inhibitors; others find that side effects are mild or temporary. Common mild side effects include dizziness, light-headedness, or faintness, especially when getting up from a lying or sitting position (rising slowly may help); drowsiness; gastrointestinal problems; appetite changes; muscle twitching; restlessness; and sexual difficulties. If side effects are a problem, tell your doctor. Your dosage or dosage schedule can be adjusted to minimize them.

Side effects that should be reported to your doctor include dark urine, diarrhea, severe dizziness, skin rash, swelling of the feet or lower legs, unusual nervousness, or yellow eyes or skin.

Stop taking this medication and get immediate emergency help if any of these side effects occur: severe chest pain, enlarged pupils, severe headache, increased sensitivity of eyes to light, nausea and vomiting, stiff or sore neck, unusually rapid or slow heartbeat, or unusual sweating.

If beneficial effects do not appear immediately, be patient. In some cases, it can take as long as four to six weeks for an MAO inhibitor to begin to work. Follow your doctor's advice closely; don't stop taking your medication unless your doctor advises you to do so. Your patience may be rewarded by a significant improvement in how you feel and function at home, socially, and on the job.

Table 1
Foods, Beverages, and Drugs to Avoid

The following foods, beverages, and drugs must be avoided while you are taking MAO inhibitors *and for two weeks after discontinuing use:*

Meat and fish

- Meats prepared with tenderizers
- Meat extracts
- Smoked or pickled fish
- Beef or chicken liver
- Dry sausage (Genoa salami, hard salami, pepperoni, bologna)

Fruits and vegetables

- Canned figs
- Broad bean (fava bean) pods
- Bananas and avocados (especially if overripe)

Dairy products

- Cheese and foods containing cheese, such as cheese crackers and pizza (cottage cheese and cream cheese are allowed)
- Yogurt and sour cream

Beverages

- Beer, red wine, and other alcoholic beverages

Miscellaneous

- Soy sauce
- Yeast extract (including brewer's yeast in large quantities)
- Excessive amounts of chocolate and caffeine
- Spoiled or improperly refrigerated, handled, or stored protein-rich foods such as meats, fish, and dairy products
- Foods that have undergone protein changes by aging, pickling, fermentation, or smoking

Drugs

- Cold, hay fever, or sinus tablets or liquids
- Nasal decongestants (tablets, drops, or spray)
- Asthma inhalant medications
- Anti-appetite or weight-reducing preparations
- "Pep" pills or stimulants
- Narcotics, including cocaine

WHAT YOU SHOULD KNOW ABOUT TRICYCLIC ANTIDEPRESSANTS

Tricyclic antidepressants are used to treat depression, certain anxiety disorders, and other illnesses.

Beneficial Effects

Tricyclic antidepressants can help ease the symptoms of anxiety and depression. Because tricyclic antidepressants can be sedating, they can be taken at bedtime to promote sleep and alleviate the insomnia and fatigue that many people with anxiety and depression feel.

Guidelines

In many cases, the medication need only be taken once a day at bedtime. You may need to take it for several weeks before you begin to feel better. Do not change the dose (take less or more) or the frequency (take it more or less often), or stop taking the medication without talking to your doctor. Your doctor has helped you select the most appropriate drug and dosage, and it is important that you follow the doctor's instructions carefully for best results.

Precautions

- Tricyclic antidepressants can be sedating; so you may feel drowsy or less alert than usual. Therefore, you should know how you react to this medication before you drive a car or operate any machinery.

- Because this medication can add to the effects of alcohol or other central nervous system depressants (drugs that slow down the nervous system), check with your doctor before drinking alcoholic beverages or taking any other drugs.

- If you are pregnant, intend to become pregnant, or are breast-feeding, inform your doctor before taking this medication.

- Tell your doctor if you are allergic to or taking any medication, either prescription or nonprescription.

- Tell your doctor if you have glaucoma, urinary retention, or heart problems.

Possible Side Effects

Many patients experience side effects while taking this medication. Such effects usually occur early in treatment and often disappear within a few weeks. The most common side effects are drowsiness, dry mouth, dizziness or light-headedness, headache, tremor or sweating, urinary retention, and constipation. These effects indicate that the medication is working. Let your doctor know if you experience any of them. Your dosage can be adjusted to minimize them, or a different tricyclic can be prescribed. If you experience any severe or unusual symptoms, call your doctor right away. Despite the side effects, it is worth continuing with the medication because of the relief you may experience in time.